CHALK FACE MUSE

POETRY AS A FOREIGN LANGUAGE

Poems connected with
English as A Foreign or Second language

Edited by Martin Bates

POETRY AS A FOREIGN LANGUAGE
is published by
White Adder Press, Lynn Cottage,
East Linton, East Lothian EH40 3DA

Printed by
T.J. International, Padstow, Cornwall

ISBN 0 9520827 3 X

Book design, layout, illustrations by

Jan Tabraham
Illustration and Graphic Design

36 Rodney Street,
Edinburgh EH7 4DX
tel: 0131 557 4493

CONTENTS

PREFACE

Most of the poems in this book arose out of a competition, which was also an investigation into the possibilities of linking EFL and poetry. The White Adder EFL Poetry Competition was held at the end of 1998 and attracted entries from or set in over 35 countries.

The competition entries were judged by Donald Adamson, John Daniel and Jane Spiro, and the winners selected from a short-list by Jo Shapcott. They were:

First prize:	John Kay:	*Moshav*
Second Prize:	John Haynes	*Camouflage*
Runners-up:	Dona Luongo Stein:	*In Munich*
	Carole Bromley:	*Home Tuition, 1980*

The following poems were highly commended by the judges:

Gerry Abbott:	*Visiting Expert*
Gavin Bantock:	*Twenteen*
Nick Blair:	*The Round Pond, Kensington Gardens*
Tim Cassidy:	*Little Room in Kyushu*
FJ Dale:	*Language School, April*
Jeremy Jacobson:	*The Post-Modern Lecture*
Olivia McMahon:	*English Language Conference in Dublin*
Christine McNeill:	*Words in his Pocket*
Joan Michelson:	*Lessons in Humanity: 1973-1998*
Mike Ramsden:	*Poetry as a Foreign Language*
Cecilia Rossi:	*Slug*
Jim Scrivener:	*Wolves*
Robert Seatter:	*The Bright Dresses*
Irene Soriano Flórez:	*The White Room*
Michael Swan:	*Meditation on a Lecture on Pragmatics*
Vivienne Vermes:	*The English Lesson*

In addition to the competition poems, there are a number of poems previously published or from other sources (including poems by the judges).

Our sincere thanks are due to the many people and organisations who helped both by supporting and publicising the competition and by advising on the development of the anthology.

The idea of an international EFL poetry competition was suggested by Donald Adamson, following successful local ones among his students in Finland. We thank him together with Jane Spiro and John Daniel for their invaluable support and advice; Patrick Early, Olivia McMahon, and many others who have helped shape the project.

For help with the competition, we thank the staff of the British Council ELT Unit and Literature Department, Eric Glendinning and Edinburgh University IALS, Tony Duff, Jean Peto and International House, Susan Norman and SEAL, the staff of IATEFL and ELGazette, and many others too numerous to name.

Special thanks to Katie, Annabel, Madeline and Alexander for moral and logistical support.

Finally, we thank all those who entered the competition for their wonderful enthusiasm and imagination, as well as those teachers and parents who encouraged the writers of the future to enter.

* * *

Acknowledgements: previously published poems

Our thanks are due to the following copyright holders for permission to publish their poems:

Colin McKay for *The Man with the Umbrella* from *Cold Night Lullaby* (Chapman Publishing, Edinburgh 1998)

Edwin Morgan for *The First Men on Mercury* from *Collected Poems* (Carcanet Press Ltd, Manchester, 1990)

Martin Bates' poems *Abbas is already in China* and *The Broken Glasses* are from *Wounded Lion* (Redbeck, 1998)

Sarah Lawson for *Foreign Expert* and *Doing Donne* from *Down where the Willow is Washing her Hair* (Hearing Eye, London, 1995)

John Liddy for *Language Lesson* from *Wine and Hope-Vino y Esperanza* (Archione Editorial, Madrid, 1999)

As Teacher, as Learner is adapted from the poem of that title published in *Spoken Language* (CILT, 1986)

The Idiomatic English Teacher previously appeared in *Modern English Teaching*, Vol. 4, No. 3, July 1995 (Longman)

From the spoken English of Iraq - Part One previously appeared in *The Rialto*, Norwich

INTRODUCTION

The poems in this anthology will take the reader on a voyage of exploration, among the many worlds where English is learned, taught and spoken as a foreign or second language. They reveal the human face of EFL.

Reading the anthology is also a voyage of exploration along frontiers - between language-learning and poetry; between the language of the textbook and the language of life; between the certainties of experts and the complexities of the worlds they pass through, between uses of language for communicating information, expressing feelings and letting the imagination roam free.

The book may also be seen as an experiment: an enquiry into the place of creativity in language-learning and the possibilities of writing poetry in a foreign language, where even mistakes can have a poetic effect, and the dead language that EFL sometimes resembles can spring into strange life forms.

The poems have come from, are set in or inspired by many different countries. The anthology traverses continents and enables us to share the feelings of people using the language in a great diversity of situations, as teacher, learner or observer, inside and outside the classroom.

We have attempted to indicate the diversity of origins by naming a country after the authors' name at the foot of each poem. This is the setting of the poem or the place that inspired it, not necessarily the nationality of the author; nor does it represent that country *per se* but rather the author's subjective feelings about that country. Where the setting is not specific, or includes more than one country, we name the place from which the author sent us the poem.

*　　*　　*

Some of the most striking poems come from learners, including children; their writing enables the reader to view the world through their eyes and share their hopes and fears - the frustration, fascination and triumph of grappling with a strange language, gradually discovering its meanings and making them part of their own lives.

The individual voices of students show extraordinary powers of imagination and expression in the foreign language:

Only when you've felt what it's like
The wind whistling on your face
And stepping unshod on wet green grass
And wearing warm gloves on a cold day

And have eaten the very first bite
Of a huge purple grape ...

(Miguel Ángel Muñoz Lobo: *Getting the Exact Word in English*)

For some learners, the foreign language even offers a new freedom of expression that was not available in the "mother-tongue":

The new language
rose naked,
unashamed.

Devoid of origin
it unearthed the roots
exposed the seeds.

(Cecilia Rossi: *May Poem*)

As well as sharing the feelings of individual learners, as we move through the anthology, we get a glimpse of learning communities; we join in the hurly-burly of classroom interaction, its joys and sadness, the confusion of different voices, the surreal impact of textbook rituals on the human urge to communicate -

And I am going madly
With Pierre and Mimi and Jorge.
Am I bored? Am I boring?
Am I snored? Am I snoring?
Multiple choice. Fill in the blanks.

(Mavis Howard: *Opening a Window, 1974*)

We share the successes and failures to communicate, the shock of exposure and comic anticlimaxes and absurdities - and then the moments of "break-through" when 'Ideas touch down like long-delayed flights' (Leslie Stuart Tate: *ESOL*).

We listen to the voices of learners and the public and private voices of teachers, who express inner feelings about their public role: terrifying, as in Jim Scrivener: *Wolves* ; funny (James Munro: *Helen*), poignant (Mavis Howard: *Opening a Window - 1974*). Teachers reflect on their role as intermediaries between cultures, questioning the ownership of the language - 'These words are not my own' (Dave Hill: *Philology*) and the meaning of what they do:

... as if the world cannot be trusted.
Nor can we. If I'm part problem,
part solution, what's to teach?

(Tim Cassidy: *Teaching English for Special Purposes*)

While some poems touch on the conflicts of classroom encounters, others reveal an impressive range of fellow-feeling between teachers and students. There is Christine McNeill's wonderful poem in memory of a language teacher (*Words in his Pocket.*). Some poems celebrate "Out of Class Activities" - amorous or otherwise (as in the poem of that name by Dave Hill). Sometimes we wonder who is the teacher, who the learner (Jenny King: *Lesson*).

Many poems reveal how closely the exchange of language is linked to cultural interchange. While struggling to come to terms with the sounds and shapes of the foreign language, the learner is often also faced with an unfamiliar culture, in conditions which may involve isolation, uprooting or exile. Several poems express sympathy for the exile or the outsider, such as Nick Blair's *The Round Pond, Kensington Gardens.*

This feeling of uprooting and estrangement may be true also for the expatriate teacher (e.g. Tim Cassidy: *Janice's Spanish Album*).

Other poems engage with the language itself - words which become focus for feelings between people (e.g. John Kay: *It wouldn't do*) - moments when the learner language takes on a creative life of its own (Gavin Bantock: *Twenteen*).

Poetry, which stands at some remove from day-to-day relationships and roles, also enables us to view afresh the absurdities of textbook language (e.g. Vivienne Vermes: *The English Lesson*) and the solemnities of experts (e.g. Olivia McMahon: *English Language Conference in Dublin*).

* * *

Most of the poems in the anthology were originally entered for the White Adder International EFL Poetry Competition (1998). The organiser and judges of the competition were people who worked in EFL but also wrote poetry and felt a strong need to encourage creativity in the use of the language, within and beyond the classroom. We also believed that many teachers would share this feeling; some would include creative writing in their language-teaching or would be poets themselves, since the life of the migrant TEFLer mediating between languages and between cultures would be a suitable context for writing.

In selecting the short-list of poems entered for the competition, the judges looked for qualities such as a sense of form, including sound, sensitivity to language, wholeness and coherence of conception, freshness and avoidance of cliché (or fresh use of cliché in poems drawing on textbook language). Although the majority of entrants were native-speakers of English, it was heartening to note that some of the short-listed poems were by non-native-speakers, including children.

The anthology follows the same lines but extends its scope; our aim is to represent the fascinating range of voices expressing many different points of view - learning, teaching, living with EFL - and to combine variety of outlook or inspiration with sincerity and an imaginative feel for language.

Reading, judging and editing the poems has been a source of great pleasure and also of curiosity and surprise. It was an education for us indeed and demolished quite a few assumptions about the limitations on language use by learners. Who would have thought that so many non-native-speakers (some of them children) could write so well and so variously in the foreign language, expressing feelings of such immediacy and vividness? How is it that "errors" like "That old man has waterfalls in his eyes" (Roger Mortimore: *Touch it Again, Sam)* can read like poetic leaps of the imagination?

While we cannot claim that the anthology represents the whole world of EFL, the distribution of the poems is interesting. Certain regions seem particularly fertile for Poetry as a Foreign Language: Spain, Eastern Europe, Japan and, perhaps most surprisingly, the Arabian Peninsula, which produced some fine poems about expatriate life and the meeting of cultures.

* * *

The book is organised into 14 sections which reflect the themes of the poems and the points of view they express. These cover three areas: learning, language and socio-cultural settings.

Section 1 - The Experience of Learning - contains poems by learners and teachers, native- and non-native-speakers, on the pleasures, pitfalls and excitements of taking possession of the foreign language.

Section 2 - Classroom Interaction - takes us into the arena of learning with its dynamism, humour and tensions, mingling a variety of voices.

In Section 3 - The Teacher Reflects - the focus moves from learner to teacher: what it feels like to be a teacher (sometimes under inspection!), what questions arise about the nature of the job and the language that is being taught.

Section 4 - Language and Identity - takes us further into the question of what is being learned and taught: whose language is it? What meanings, conscious and sub-conscious, does it carry for the individual and the community?

In Section 5 - A Meeting of Cultures - we explore the cultural settings in which the language-learning takes place and the coming together of very different worlds with humorous, disturbing or moving effects.

Section 6 - Appeals to Language - contains poems in which words themselves - words between people - take on a heightened meaning as focus for feelings and thoughts.

In Section 7 - The Ghost of the Textbook - EFL practitioners look askance at the strangely ritualised language of textbooks and classroom drills, comparing it ironically with real life situations in which language has a more urgent purpose.

The poems in Section 8 - A Meeting of Languages - give food for thought on the effects of language "error" - where one language collides with another - to comic and sometimes strangely poetic effect.

Section 9 - Enter the Expert - continues in humorous or satirical vein - casting a sceptical eye on the expert who attempts to make the real world fit preconceived opinion.

Section 10 - Migration and Exile - reveals the feelings of less privileged travellers than those in the previous section, refugees, exiles, immigrants or outsiders; people uprooted and thrust into alien worlds made more confusing by the strange language, which combines risk with chances of security.

In Section 11- The Second Person - the poems express intimate feelings between people brought together in the strange world of TEFL - feelings of love, friendship or loss.

Section 12 - Expatriate Life - has poems of humour or poignancy of particular interest to people whose involvement with EFL has taken them far from their home country.

Some of the poems in Section 13 - Language Play - are written directly for teaching - rhymes and word-patterns to demonstrate features of the language, such as idioms.

The final Section - 14 Dreaming in a Foreign Language - includes some poems from learners which explore the language's creative potential - images and reflections.

The section following the poems, listing them according to theme, variety of writing or poetic feature, is a guide to selecting poems for reading or for creative writing, using the poems as models or starting-points.

* * *

While the origins of these poems are very diverse, there is a common thread that unites them and that runs across boundaries geographic and human - a fascination with and curiosity about language - what it expresses and conceals, what happens when languages, communities and cultures come into contact. The authors of these poems care about language and about people. Poetry enables them to express their thoughts and feelings, combining the intimate and the public, about what they are doing with words.

The discipline of EFL may seem far removed from poetry, with its medley of different voices that sometimes shout, sometimes whisper, sometimes beg in vain for an audience, but have been known to shake thrones. The public view of poetry and poets in the cultures of the countries where English has been spoken longest may be less positive than in those other places where EFL is taught (Mike Ramsden: *Poetry as a Foreign Language*). As the discipline of EFL has developed over the past 40 years, there has been a movement away from literature towards more easily definable uses of the language, more obviously relevant to learning needs and objectives. Recently, however, there has been a revival of interest in the creative and expressive potential of language, as an important ingredient in the learning process, since much of the linguistic material emerging from the narrowly utilitarian approach is so bland or dull and, as we feel these poems show, the learner has an urge, even at an early stage, to play and joke and be creative in the new language.

We hope that these poems will both amuse people engaged with EFL and also reveal truths about the experience that are outside, but complementary to, the discourses of TEFL methodology and applied linguistics. Perhaps the poet can perform a useful function in those disciplines akin to that of the court jester. The poems about textbook language and about the influence of "experts" (Sections 7 and 9) seem to be doing this; indeed, some of the jesters at the court of ELT have also earned distinction there for their wisdom; their ability to laugh at themselves is a healthy sign.

In selecting, grouping and sequencing these poems, we have been struck by their energy and variety and by the way the poems originating in very different places, when placed together, seem to take on a life of their own and to start talking to one another. The aim of this book is firstly to give pleasure but also to encourage the conversation between poem and poem, between EFL and poetic language, to continue and grow beyond its bounds.

1 EXPERIENCE OF LEARNING

Will I fly with English
out of this white room?

The White Room

I am now feeling
like a lost camel
in the Sahara Desert.
I am very young
and I've got a lot of things
to learn.

Sometimes
I think:
I don't know anything
I should go to my house
and begin to study.
But, then, I think
Why? A lot of the time
knowledge flies after studying.
Will I fly with English
out of this white room?

Irene Soriano Flórez - Spain

About Getting the Exact Word in English

Only when you've felt what it's like:
The wind whistling on your face
And stepping unshod on wet green grass
And wearing warm gloves on a cold day
And have eaten the very first bite
Of a huge purple grape,
Only then will you know what it is like
To grasp the exact word and make
What you want to say better
All this happens of a sudden
And then it is again
That anxious moment of search
Which flows into that moment
When you can clench
The exact word again
And so goes language
As a vicious circle that holds you.

Miguel Ángel Muñoz Lobo - Spain

Other Languages

There they really do things
differently - cucumber-sliced
slivers of spiced agglutination.
A thousand toxic pixies
stagger through parataxis.
Those antonyms and triple
negatives! Such sleight
of tongue and tweezer-tight
control! Angels dancing
on a velar fricative!

But if, through tip-toe
balance, and creeper-clung
grip, you survive that steamy
jungle, the retroflex rains,
piranha plosives, the doom-
clogged rivers of hollow
logs and supersegmental
squids, one day clouds begin
to swirl away, and mountains
of meaning brilliantly loom.

David Kerr - Botswana

A Trip without End

English is as interesting as
a trip to something you don't know;
you are introduced to it when you are young.
This is a lost world for you.

You observe the beautiful scenery
but you don't know how to interpret it;
hear some sounds
that you have never heard before
without wanting to think
they are going to unite.

It's a long and difficult road
that will never finish,
but you cast your fears aside
and forget them.
In time you'll find the way.

So when you feel that hope
you will be strong, and ask yourself. Why?
Why did I have to do this trip?
When you advance you'll see an answer
that you expected but didn't reach.

Every one of us, must find this answer,
and follow. On this trip there will be

other trips, but none will have a final ●

Each may choose their ● ● ●

Ana Jiménez Martín - Spain

In a Small English Room

In a small English room
Of an old Vilnius school
Overlooking the town
On the restless Neris,
Smiling Queen from the wall
Greets a shy little girl.
With an armful of books
And a pen in her hand.

In a small English room
Of an old Vilnius school
Overlooking the town
On the restless Neris,
Lithuanian girl's
Writing back to her friends,
In Shakespearian tongue
And Čiurlionian mind.

Genovaitė Snuviškienė - Lithuania

Roofs

A number of roofs
after each other
through the window.
A thin layer of snow
on the red wavy bricks.

Grey November afternoon at 3 p.m.
A few minus degrees.
The blue moment.

Students writing in English
about healthy eating habits
and a good life.

The blue moment turning
to darkness.
Our minds singing their autumn song.

Riitta Venola - Finland

Linguistic Clock

striking in my ribcage
that half-known
language
leaves
me dizzy.

Footprints on an evening sky,
blood and cosmic sand;
sober steps along
a wine-dark path.

This lunar clock cheats me tonight.
Still, against the odds,
I measure worlds
in world-speech;

and insist.

Borivoje Baltezarevic - Scotland

Words

I like words.
I like Finnish words.
I like English words.
What is a word?

Words sound good, taste good,
look good, feel good.
Words are exciting and surprising.

"Feel" is a beautiful word.
I also like "why".
I love the world of words!

Riitta Venola - Finland

New Shoes

New shoes - seen on display
And fallen in love with immediately
I try them on
They fit just perfectly
These new shoes

I am very excited
They look so nice
I wear them on every possible occasion
These new shoes

The shoes are hurting
I struggle but I cannot take them off
Walking barefoot - impossible
I want to give them up
These new shoes

I put them on again
I bear the pain
I keep walking on them
These new shoes

I can see where the blisters have been
My skin is harder thicker now
No aches no blisters anymore
The shoes are walked in now
And they fit - **these new shoes**

Elizabeth Bjorkman and Franke David - England

Sound Barrier

Languages can keep their distance
From those labouring to learn 'em
Putting up a stout resistance
Causing aches from mouth to sternum.

English has defensive features
Sure to daunt the bravest learner
(Thus pronunciation teachers
Are assured a lifelong earner).

Dipthongs, tripthogs - muscle-busters
Certainties to mispronounce
Crooked consonantal clusters
Waiting on the weak to pounce

Vowels which may be weak or strong
Depending on the stress or rhythm
Not to mention words so long
That even natives struggle with 'em.

All this means an aching tongue
And vocal chords forever sore
Palpitations in the lung
In other words, the marks of war.

Roger Berry - Hong Kong

Learning a Language

is like doing a jigsaw puzzle
of a million pieces
with a picture that keeps changing.
It's like getting lost in a foreign city
without a map.
It's like playing tennis without a ball,
like being an ant in a field of grasshoppers.
It's being an acrobat with a broken leg,
an actor without a script,
a carpenter without a saw,
a storyteller without a middle or an end.

But then gradually
it's like being out in the early morning
with the mists lifting.
It's like a chink of light under a door,
like finding the glove you were looking for,
catching the train you thought you were going to miss,
getting an unlooked-for present,
exchanging a smile.

And then one day it's like riding a bicycle
very fast downhill.

Olivia McMahon - Scotland

Brain Waves

Brain wave, brain wave,
What kind of wave is a brain wave?
Does it ebb and flow like the waves of the sea
Incessantly?

There are brain waves inside my head right now
Ebbing and flowing with every tide.
Smashing and crashing away inside
My head.

Brain waves, brain waves
Please slow to a ripple and take me to shore.
Cease all the thrashing, the lashing, the roar.
Let me be captain of my soul
Once more in control.
I need to be able to study, to think.
Right now I'm on the perilous brink
Of collapse.

Oh, brain waves have mercy, be tranquil, be calm.
You do me injustice, you do me such harm.
How can I pass an exam or a test
In such unrest?

Su Taher - Egypt

The Maze

English Spelling.
You are the Maze
That I try my best
To find my way through.

Sometimes I see scorpions,
At other times
I see the bright rays of sunlight
In the Maze.

Your silent letters are written,
You have interesting doubles,
Your letters ring different sounds.
You fascinate me Spelling Maze!

English Spelling
You are certainly
A fascinating Maze!

Dumisani Sally Ndlovu - Zimbabwe

To Travel

I want to travel,
To see new places,
To enjoy myself,
To go here and there,
To tell my friends
How many countries I know.
But I don't want to learn,
I don't want the work
Of learning new languages,
To communicate with people.
What I really want is to travel.
And when I come back
My friends will ask me
How was my trip,
I will answer "wonderful"!
I saw churches and museums
That I don't know the names of,
I had a drink with someone
Whom I couldn't speak with,
I had a guide book
Which I couldn't read.
So I stayed in the hotel
Wondering how wonderful it is
To be abroad.

Edjane Harris - Senegal

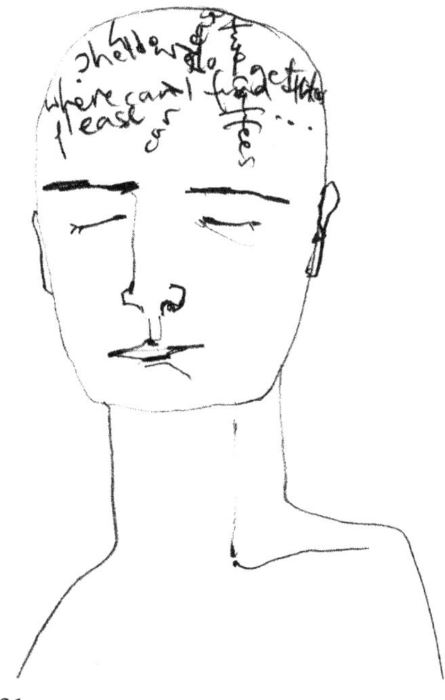

English & I

English is the language of the world;
English is the world itself;
English is the books I read;
English is the film I've seen;
The music that I listen to;
The picture I'm showing you;
The glass I'm drinking knowledge of.
All I do is caused by love.
English is a window to the world
And the way I say this word
Shows my power over you
And my possibilities too.
I use it with pleasure and from love,
I think it's easy and rough.
English is a ghost that haunts me
Day and night, at home and in class.
English is around me, every season that I see.
It's the snow that falls in winter,
It's the leaf that grows in spring,
It's the summer on the beach,
It's the autumn that's so rich.

Teodora Petrova Ivanova - Bulgaria

A New World

Suddenly all is quiet, the men have left;
And with them the cases and crates, boxes and all.
The rooms stand bare.

In the midst of the empty silence sits Anna on the floor,
staring out at the falling snow.
She hugs her newly received African doll;
clueless as to the future that lies ahead.

The engines come to a gradual standstill, the plane has landed;
The pitch black complexion of the field staff
is baffling enough,
but it is the overwhelming heat that truly slaps her in the face
as she steps off the plane.
Yet it is with the uninhibited heart of a child
that Anna takes all this in.

The car ride to their new home takes her
across the savannah, beyond the Rift Valley,
into the high plains. A new world.

Anna stands in front of her new class, watching wordless,
as the teacher utters words alien to her,
an obscure language;
And mutely listens, watchful for any sound or syllable
that might ring a bell,
but understands not a word.
The teacher motions for her to sit down, and class begins.

And behold, no longer is English unfathomable;
Anna studies hard, learns fast, and soon blends in.

But alas, the child now fails to remember
the language of her ancestors, her relations past and present,
the language of yesteryear.

Merja Ryhaven - Finland

2 CLASSROOM INTERACTION

And every word living and breathing ...

A Special Case

In this special case
the teacher writing poems
the students working on their own.
A pleasant case.

Writing. Looking for ideas.
Looking for words.
Making sensible sentences.

That's what they are doing.
That's what I am doing.

Riitta Venola - Finland

Opening a Window - 1974

What am I doing? Mohammad?
You're opening the window.
Good. Ute? ... writing on the blackboard.
Good. Suki? ... looking in your bag.
And I am going madly
With Pierre and Mimi and Jorge.
Am I bored? Am I boring?
Did I snored? Did I snoring?
Multiple Choice. Fill in the blanks.
Multiple choice they are adoring.
Blank blank blank ...

But today we'll do drama
Blank blank what drama? ... Well Sami ...
And what is Violeta doing?
She's sleeping. Damn Violeta. Bioleta.
She's sitting in the corner
Muttering in Spanish about going to the toilet.
Is she shooting up?
They are giggling. Are you giggling Violeta?
No you're sleeping.

A Man for All Seasons. Explain.
Jailer (explain): a plain simple man
Just want to keep out of trouble.
Improvisation. What what?
We act Françoise we act ... ah oui.
In threes. The husband the wife the jailer.
She comes to persuade him to tell.
Yes in threes make the space small.
You've never been in prison Sven?
You've watched television. Imagine.
Yes we're into it. Good Mohammad.
And Violeta is sleeping.
Shall we wake her and tell her?
Violeta you're in prison.

Violeta is screaming. She is running.

Your register. Please amend.
Free place. Star the third column.
Refugee. Chile.

Mavis Howard - England

English Lesson

We are doing Chapter 6: Hobbies, *I like doing...*

Roberto is playful and wants to talk about sex in cars
and gear sticks. We lose ourselves in body parts:
engine, carburettor, *vroom, vroom.*

Carla likes cooking, the *gnocchi*
her grandmother taught her how to make - a whole day set
aside, potatoes in piles, all the family peeling.
Her fingers forgetful of typewriter keys.

Giancarlo bicycles twenty kilometres every Sunday
(we imagine his overfed thighs in lycra and laugh).
He lists all the cups he won when the weekend was just
one long white road, his podgy hands making circles,
his moustached mouth the whirring of spokes.

Gianni goes back to his village, kisses his seven
little sisters, loves checking his row of reddening tomatoes.
He wears different shoes, screwing his face up at
buckled black leather. No briefcase. No boss.

Francesca likes going to the mountains, the lakes, the sea -
wherever her friends have houses. We are all invited.
When you open the windows all the houses have
beautiful views, and there is *panetone* for breakfast.

Franco plays cards in the bar with his friends.
Same bar, same friends: every evening playing poker
at Vittorio's place. He counts the years on his fingers
as if he had never counted before.

Lucia says she cries all weekend, every weekend -
since Massimo left her. She sits in the flat and cries.
There is nothing else to do.

The silence pulls at her words, dangling cut-out and
foreign on the air, begging to be mistakable:
a disappearing trick against the classroom's white walls.

Then Roberto claps his hands. He meant to say
he likes practising English. We all groan.

Robert Seatter - Italy

Doing "Used to": A Bad Day at the Chalk-Face

I used to drink whisky
I don't drink whisky any more. I drink Seven-Up.
Do I still drink whisky?
No, I don't.
I used to but I don't now.
I used to be strong.
I'm not strong anymore.
Am I still strong?
Correct. I'm not strong. I'm weak.
I used to be strong.
I used to be young.
I used to be married.
TAKE UP TEXT. WHAT IT USED TO BE LIKE IN THE SIXTIES
Twiggy used to have nice legs.
Twiggy used to be a model.
We used to make love not war -
Teacher, teacher, what mean?
Everyone used to like each other, Ahmed,
And there were no wars in the sixties.
Shall we move on?
We used to stay out all night.
We used to have long hair -
Teacher, teacher, girl-boys?
We used to wear flowers in our hair.
Teacher, teacher, I see boys with rings on TV.
Haram, haram!

ROUND THE CLASS
I used to visit my village
I used to see my grandfather
I used to play football
I used to fish
I used to be a good boy.

Mike Ramsden - Muscat Oman

Helen

Come on, Mister -
admit you missed her ...

Missed her?!?

Mister! What's this? You're late again - look!
And don't say you haven't corrected my book?
Those are new boots! Nice! But look at your hair -
And where's that pullover I like you to wear?

Mister! Not grammar! Let's go for a walk!
Or see a video! Or just sit and talk!
Mister! Say 'Please' when you ask *me* a question!
Mister - *me* cause you *stress*? Me?! May I make a suggestion -

With your permission, of course - my I speak? -
You only ask *me* one small question per week -
If that - no, it's true! you always ask her -
What?! No, I'd *die* before calling you 'Sir'!

You're losing it, Mister. Suggestion? Oh yes -
I've forgotten - that's your fault - you won't let me express
My thoughts and feelings, my dreams - you just frown -
The suggestion? Oh yes, Mister - you should Calm Down,

Stay Cool and Get Real - What's this 'Page 21'
When we're chatting and laughing and having some fun,
This 'Page 21, books closed, question 3'?
Mister!! Did you see TONY last night on TV?!

Yes, I admit
It's less than bliss
This peace and quiet.
Miss you, Miss.

James Munro - Greece

Always More to Learn

Keep your head down and listen,
monitor, watch, help them
across the silences,
classroom conversations.

Why do you have separate two hot and cold tap?
Why always you eat so much fatfood,
chips chips chips ever time chips?
My host father always he talk about
the fogging weather
now I understand fogging
I am kernackered.
And why you cook apple please?
A flat dish no so very convenient for eat soup?
In England you not eat many rice?
And the women of your village,
they often take by crocodile?
Yes, a tea junction, the place
for motorists to halt and take tiffin.

But I don't think you understand

The. Meaning.

ultimate

fragments

Ho-ho?

Ah?

The teacher is like ...?

The learner is like ...?

Like you teacher ...?

Teacher learn you ...?

But I really don't think you understand!

Stereotype? Yes, that one very good make. I have at home. Is Sony, is Japan.

No, I don't think so, you really don't understand!!
Jorge from Chile, sitting right here in our classroom, slowly
pulls off his sweater,
his shirt,
his vest.
We see the scars, the burn marks.
The class gapes, gasps.
Silence of complete understanding, his silence, the hurt in his eyes.

Charles Hadfield - England

"Thuh"

The classroom holds the silence like a spell.
Eyes tangling along the print, a flick
back, and then along again. A drama,
and Ahrfan understands the drama well.

Behind his massive European Art
he gets his tongue in place between his lips
as for the English *thuh* and blasts a fart
that click-clicks thickly like a giant jacket zip.

Miss Stamper's heels and swerving mini-skirt
come fast to where his cheek is pressed down flat
and turned away. Her whirlpool specs scowl at
the gap jerking between his belt thong and his shirt.

The pictures of the Vikings on the wall,
the squares, circles, numbers, symbols, stars, space,
Our Code of Conduct, Finished Work, A4 -
these hold the very classroom bricks and roof in place.

John Haynes - England

Poetry Hour

Come class, I said, it's time for a poem
Time to show what you can do,
I wrote one yesterday morning
And if I can, then you all can too.

Can we be minimal? said Jo from the corner,
I HATE READING, will that suffice?
You can try, but remember the judges,
They might think that rather concise.

Only 40 lines! commented Laura,
How can I keep it to that?
With difficulty I thought, but kept silent,
The endless way you like to chat.

They sweated and strained for an hour
And scratched and scribbled in their book
They looked out the window and sighed and looked glum
Till finally I had a quick look.

There on the page was some English,
Not "correct", not "normal", not "right"
But every word living and breathing
And dancing around with delight.

Can you check this please, Teacher? they asked me
Have I written as you would have done?
No, I replied, quite proudly.
You haven't, not a single one.

English is not mine for the giving,
It may have been mine by birth,
But it is endlessly changing and growing
To reach all the peoples on earth.

So write what you like, keep inventing,
In poetry nothing's "just so"
And if you find a new expression to use
Don't hesitate, just let me know!

Heather Oxley - Italy

3 THE TEACHER REFLECTS

As teacher, as learner ...

Lessons in Humanity: 1973-1998

Teaching EFL I listen mostly.
This began the year we lost Allende.
My class was filled with refugees from Chile.

The students had a lot of things to tell me.
The world they'd seen: a new democracy.
Teaching them, I learned to listen mostly.

Pinochet sent his henchmen for Allende.
Thousands disappeared: their democracy.
That class was packed with refugees from Chile.

They hid the worst. I helped with phrasing mostly,
style for official forms, linguistic niceties.
Teaching the Chilenos, I listened mostly.

I learned: Victor Jara went down singing,
though his hands were broken by the junta.
I lived that year as if my home were Chile

and I expected Britain to protect me
until I had a home beyond Pinochet.
My class was filled with refugees from Chile.
Teaching EFL I listened mostly.

Joan Michelson - England

from **As Teacher, as Learner**

(An EFL teacher enrols for beginners' Arabic)

As teacher anxious to give them their money's worth,
Reluctant to stop once started.
The 50 minutes grow, become 55, 60.
How time flies!
As learner the hour blinks slowly by, sly references to watch,
Only 35 minutes gone, only 5 to go, now 4, now 3. . .

As teacher careless of appearance:
Hair barely combed, shoes unpolished, finger-nails short of impeccable.
What does it matter? It's the teaching that counts.
As learner the idle noticing of details,
What was she wearing the other day? A lilac dress, I think.
Skirt a little tight, maybe, but, all the same,
Today she is better dressed. Yes.

As teacher keen to get through a substantial amount,
So pushing on to keep boredom at bay
Avoiding silence at all costs.
As learner the luxury of doing nothing, while teacher writes it up.
Delighting in strange sounds, in simple communicative acts
"Can you come to tea tomorrow?" "No, but the day after, Inshallah."
The pleasure of saying "Here is my passport", "This is not my camel."

As teacher wary of red herrings,
Suppressing a temptation to talk of pubs and Coronation Street.
As learner eager for trappings to clothe the language in:
Who talks to who about what, and when? What do Arabs do all day?

As teacher, like a hostess, happy when all are there,
But not too fussed if one or two are missing.
The others will have more of me - more chance to practise.

As learner more conscious of the gulf that separates teacher from taught
The comfort of belonging to a group.
Panic as numbers dwindle, and feeling of abandonment.
The awful possibility of being the only one.

As teacher teaching a class of imaginary people who are:
Confident, intelligent, industrious, serious, critical and impatient.
As learner lazy, timid, vulnerable, and rather stupid,
Craving niceness, tolerance, encouragement, and entertainment.

Human at last.

Olivia McMahon - Scotland

Wolves

She taught as if she was stepping
over snakes she couldn't see; as if

she stood alone, in a clearing, in a
forest, on a moonless late night, knowing

for certain (though not from howls
or snorted breath or from the soft

pawing of the earth) that all
around her, circled, waiting, eyes focussed

coldly, greenly, hidden
among the trees, the wolves

were massing.

Jim Scrivener - Hungary

Lesson

The woman stands up, stretches,
gold against the pink wall.
She's been telling me a story
concerning the Urdu for "banana"
and the English shopkeeper
piecing it out for an Asian customer.
We laugh together,
enjoy the tangled thread of speech.
"Orright," she says. "Next week. Orright,"
as I push papers into the lesson folder,
fish out the car keys.

Outside I come across Granny,
cotton garments billowing round her thinness
as she takes a little sun.
I nod. She puts her hands together, comes close,
takes mine between them, teaching me a gesture
beneath her bony smile.
We stand close, having
no word in common,
conversing silently where light
slips past the housing scheme's flagged entrance
and glints the silver speckles on her shoulder.
My student glances, curious, from the window.

At last she steps away
still smiling and I leave
a little more acquainted with this language
that makes me hold my tongue,
till as I back and turn, she waves me off
as though not I but she were the one
who profited.

Jenny King - England

Teaching English for Special Purposes

It does not mean what it has meant
to a thousand scarred or charred with
flame that clings, but when cadets smile

tea-stained teeth in my direction, I know
they understand what shells are for.
It is only language they are learning.

F-15s amuse with bombs on video,
a test-day treat. But peace only lasts
while we are watching. Soon someone

has insulted someone's origin,
city, region, race or tribe, doubted
his faith, honour or intelligence,

got the place he should have had by right.
Before I know it, war reigns, chairs fly,
pens and rulers, anything that hurts.

Up the road, the water pipe turns
at right angles from the town they say
is only Sunni. But it's preferred

not to speak of the blood-laden divide,
of the massacre twelve years old
still unreported of the other,

whose roads they leave to ruin,
till the former is resettled, leaves
them ousted from their jobs.

I think of Northern Ireland,
tallying up the toll of wrong,
pogroms of innocents,

as if the world cannot be trusted.
Nor can we. If I'm part problem,
part solution, what's to teach?

As soon as any don't matter,
and these do? *A Vietnamese, a Croat,*
and an Irishman go into a pub... .

English is not the foreign language,
nor is it all I teach, but that other
I relearn not quite by heart,

write out a thousand times,
though practice never make perfect,
and they who mark my work are nearly blind.

Tim Cassidy - Saudi-Arabia

Professional Deformation

A day of *Headway* classes taught,
The orange evening tram just caught,
I flop down on the only seat.
An elbow jabs between my ribs,
The girl next door. She turns a page.
I suppress half-intended rage,
Her book is English after all.
I hunker down and cast a glance
Sidelong.
No advert to the throng
Of the fact it interests me,
I'm really very keen to see
Just what the book she's reading is.

I watch. Her pencil traces lines.
Apparently she reads with ease.
But then she halts, her pause defines
The unknown word which undermines
Her fluency. Can I help her?
Plumpness. She underlines the word.
Shall I then say: "Signorina,
It means fatness, but not quite that,
It's less offensive, happier ..."?
She's moved on down the page. Reading.
I look up at her, wonder what
Is going on below her hat,
Her hair, her slightly furrowed brow.
Lingers. Another line. What now?
"Indugiare. Attardasi."
I am too late again. It's past.
She rattles down the page until
panties. No! Panties? No, I can't.
Not to a stranger. Pretty girl
Upon an evening tram. Not that.

David A. Hill - Italy

Language Lesson

I wanted to open their minds
To the word as I heard it
On my way to them:

"The terrorists of ...
Sorry, I'll read that again.
The territories of ..."

Open their minds to the tricks
And subtleties, shifts of emphasis,
The sly diplomacy of sounds.

Unravel the grammar of ornament,
The meaning of space on a page;
Read between the lines that lead

Into and out of the human cage.
I wanted them to know the lie,
If possible truth so that all else

Would sicken in the mouth:
Belfast crucifixion, legalised
Barbarity, kidnap victim found

Dead in the Basque country.
I wanted them to know the bullet
That bounces off the moon,

Explodes in a man's back
Going home, the key in the car
Bomb. To listen for each syllable

Like a bird-note of freedom,
Wind blowing through an empty
Classroom, something other
Than this language lesson.

John Liddy - Ireland

ESOL

The teacher does verbs.
We travel.
On the wall's a set of rules
And a blown-up atlas.
It's a forced march, flags on a map,
A series of arrivals.

Words are sails,
Skin-thin and billowing
They sing and stretch,
Run before the wind,
Odd-voiced, quirky,
They flap and tear free.

We've pegs, hoops, target circles
And a pieced-together outline;
Eager and struggling
We pull at all angles.
Taped-up, labelled, bordered,
The world is on the walls.

Learning is an action:
I see. I try. I speak.
It's present tense touching
Chanted, practised, held to a note,
An all-at-once feeling,
An engagement.
The verb repeats.
In a corner there is laughter.
Up and down voices circle print.
The walls have mouths,
Delicate, determined
They battle through check-points and barriers,
Ideas touch down like long-delayed flights.

Leslie Stuart Tate - England

The Importance of Socks

He planned his aims, his scripts, his moves, the tasks,
the seating plans, four visual aids, two games,
elicitation cues,
precisely focussed things to ask,
smart gestures to use, handouts with each student's name,
jokes to just drop in,
all timing to the minute,
links to tie it up,
and a cracking story to begin it.

But writing it out neatly, watched it sink
out of his grasp completely: vague, bland, stark,
impossible to teach,
already bathed in tutor's ink
with underlines, cool comments and red question marks.
And hidden in deep
The certain flaw to bomb it;
To leave the class quite lost
And him holding back the urge to vomit.

Teaching next day, it didn't work (of course):
He jumped around, forgot things, talked too much;
Attempted clarity
and staying in touch, but might as well
have spoken Ancient Norse. Then his tutor handed
out some compliments
and knocks and asked him to "put
greater time and thought
preparing future lessons that he taught."

He packed board pens and handouts in a box.
Had a quick Guinness. Went home. Washed his socks.

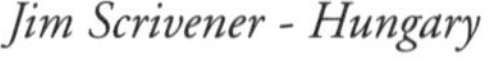

Jim Scrivener - Hungary

Renewing my Contract

Rigidly she sat there
In the circle, but not
Part of our group. Flinching
If asked to contribute, arms
Folded, determinedly willing me
Not to ask her to speak.

Unfriendly and uncooperative,
I didn't know what to do with
Her. I smiled, but her freezing
Eyes pushed me quickly away.
I wrote encouraging remarks but she
Only glared back in icy silence.

And then one day I met her
On the stairs. Embarrassed, she
Defended her absence from the
Mock Exam. "I don't know English,
Please, don't make me continue." Then
I knew I had to help her somehow.

"Come to another group, they're
studying for a different exam. I think
You'll be the best." The sparkle in her
Eyes soon died. "But I don't know them."
"They're very friendly," I assured her.
She eyed me sadly. "But I'm not."

Three months later and is this the
Same student I see before me?
Laughing as she enters, happily working
With another student? Interrupting and
Defending her point of view, chatting to
New friends? Accepted and accepting.

Rigidly I sit there,
An employee but not
One of them. Administrators
Can never understand me, arms
Folded, stubbornly fighting with
Them to let me stay another year.

Sarah Nicholson - England

4 LANGUAGE AND IDENTITY

The new language
rose naked,
unashamed ...

May Poem

May buried me in silence,
with its early dusks and first frosts.
Today it begins to stir, questions --

If the River's breeze spoke
would I not hear it?

When I was a child
one language sufficed
like bread.

My mother's words were
don't say,
hush what you feel, or think.

She meant from friends,
or men.
But it was fear (of words).

The new language
rose naked,
unashamed.

Devoid of origin
it unearthed the roots,
exposed the seeds.

First food in language,
it said,
naming my need.

Cecilia Rossi - Argentina

Slug

I walk into the darkened afternoon,
slowly fall into step
with each slurp
of old boots on wet grass or stone,

each sucking at the sole.
Yet it is not rain puddles
I dodge today
but slugs

as they slink,
all body and no limbs.
Long black pods slurring
noiselessly --

I watch them
until they call to me
from the wordless:
it is a name

they have me seek,
as hard as a mother.

The wrong words come
and slide back
as neatly as a tide
leaving no trace

of sound or breath,
no imprint on the sand.

It should lie deep as it is,
in that language of mothers,
when sounds first round
the mouth like bubbles.

Little blobs of breath
disappearing into their sand holes.
These are not crabs
but slugs.

And their mother-word
eludes me now,
three full seasons'
exile --

as if the nine months of English wet
and grey had been enough
to drown one language
in the mind.

Cecilia Rossi - Argentina

In Munich

she watches the pictures
as she sits all day long by herself
in a kitchen of cockroaches
shooting themselves in the arms

no it's the kids shooting themselves
in the arms, ankles, or between
their fingers, behind their testicles
breathing fumes no longer any good

she couldn't watch them like they're pictures
out of tune they sing what might be
"You Are My Sunshine"   redolent spring morning
fruit trees humming at once   apricot cherry

apple plum   is it latent wop syndrome
to wonder about the Germans   she thinks
part German herself   the Jewish part
maybe the Italian part too   "alles für

meinen Kindern"   that's what they always said
whether German   Italian   French   probably
Chinese too   she still walks in the history
of her people   whoever they are   they pushed

out of customs stumbling   legs numb
eyes and hands cast down wondering
where they were in kitchens with cockroaches
shooting themselves in the arms   no   that's

the kids who do the cha-cha-cha   revive the twist
all night in tight black jeans then shoot
themselves up   they squat on the edge
of Munich   she sits all day long by herself

she wants to ask you Herr Announcer
on TV   what a German is
why only Jews can be Israeli
but that's bad to ask   isn't it

now they with their homeland and Palestinians
none   though last year's el niño caused this year's
explosive spring   all the fruit trees in tune
at once sing cherry apple apricot plum

Dona Luongo Stein - USA

No Walls

There is a poet who said
My country is my language.
Then I have no country, no nation.
Why limit my world?
Why build walls?
I want to fly
In the cosmopolitan sky.
I want to be able to make people laugh
In every country, everywhere,
I want to cry with people's sadness
And be able to say
I understand you brothers.
I refuse to stay in a small room
And call it my country.
I want the whole house
And call it my world.
There is a poet who said
My country is my language
I say my language is my world
And my world is so large.

Edjane Harris - Senegal

You, and Me

I noticed in conversation the other day that
I say *they*, not *we*,
for the Scots, the English, everyone -
my family even -
and not only that, but they
say *you*, say *he*.

*

Of course, I am not - or no longer - "one of us".
(Was I ever?)
And of course I am not - or not yet - "one of them".
Sometimes I feel like a thistle grafted on
to the end of some sweet and slender
(but quite, quite thornless)
exotic stem.

*

I noticed in conversation the other day
that when I say *we* I mean *you*, my love,
and *me*.

James Munro - Greece

Philology

These words are not my own. They flow unguided
Through lips and ears. They've mixed and interbred.
They've bombed around, and bruised where they've collided,
And changed their meaning each time they've been said.

Don't talk of their descent or evolution.
Don't group them into groups. Draw me no tree.
Don't tell me to protect them from pollution.
They're global. And they don't belong to me.

They rocket out the second that I breathe them.
They cloud the air and fumigate the phone.
I nourish and inherit and bequeath them.
They pass me by. These words are not my own.

Dave Hill - Hungary

The Language Missionaries

Miss Honikman had taught us the Arabic *'ain*
and the pharynx whistle *heuh.*
Innocent postwar missionaries
armed with vowel diagrams,

we were blown by the winds of change
to the classrooms of North Africa,
(my wife said for God's sake
stop coughing like a sick cow.)

We said: English is no longer ours,
it belongs to the world,
that's why our simple mission is
to bring you strings of phonemes.

Daniel Jones was our white-maned prophet
and RP our text. Pure, classless
memoryless English
from the home (*heowm*) counties.

My best pupil, Mohammed,
all year long vocalised
those glides and practised
that tricky *schwa*,

like a virtuoso, the loud
pedal, then the soft,
the emphatic Strong forms
followed by the timid Weak.

At last we tried to talk:
It's a nice day, isn't it?
Would you like to go for a walk?
Go home, go home.

Mohammed suffered from sentence stress.
He could parrot sentence strings
but he couldn't actually talk:
he had learnt what I had taught.

The strong will never efface
the weak. That *schwa*
was a shadow dogging us
like the people of the third world.

Patrick Early - Ireland

How to say "night night"

This is the imperial language, no
doubt about it, the language of armies
advancing from Chaucer's time to Rushdie's,
the language of a service so civil
that people might not notice their country
slip away behind its back, the language
that seamed church and state in privy council
and in cloth of gold. This is the language
that said *history is now and in England.*
But me no buts, this language is over
the top, it's the language for splitting
atoms and infinitives people don't know
they had until they've had them, the language
where science is at home with stocks and shares.

Let nation speak peace unto nation, this
language I think when bats flutter at dusk
or poems or small birds sing at dawn, this
is the language of the moral maze, whose
wireless is wired to afternoon chat shows,
while its monarchy beds down with tabloid
hacks for a spot of l*ingua franca*,
and its car radio is tuned to cricket.
Welsh girls courted cockneys in this language,
and their descendants grow up polyglot.
In a genocidal century
it's still between us hopefully,
the language that tells foreign students how
to say "night night" before the cat goes out.

Janet Dubé - Wales

Speaking with English

"Hi, how you doing?" I said.
"Done in", he said.
"How come?" I said.
"Don't know", he said.
"Come, come; that's not an answer.
After all, you are a lingua franca."
"Sure. What a sickening thought ...
You know, I'm sick of being studied, of being spoken
and mistaken; I'm sick of songs and calls, and
e-mails; of everything written in me. Poetry! Ha,
poetry! They want poetry when I just like plain
chatting so much. You know, I've grown international
i.e. an expatriate, when all I want to be is - well, a
language. Damn!"
"Come, come," I said. "I forbid
A second such pathetic slip.
You know you have to ...
Keep on keeping ... a stiff ... upper lip."

Rositza Alexandrova - Bulgaria

5 A MEETING OF CULTURES

Right to left,
left to right, our hands
met in the middle ...

The Coffee Bar

I was standing at the "La Titane" drinking French coffee without sugar
when he came up to me and said "Hello there again".
Looking round I thought ... a student ... quite mature!
His name, long forgotten, was it Jean or was it Jake?
"How are you?" I replied in English
thinking "So much for my break!"

He said it was nice to see me but he hadn't found a job yet.
I remembered - unemployed and retraining a year back,
men looking for work that they just couldn't get.
Eager to talk he continued "It's hard! - Are you busy working?"
Asking myself what his name was I said
"Yes, the coffee keeps me going".

Thanking the lady there serving, leaving centimes in a pile
I was wondering what to say next when he said
"I enjoyed your classes - I'd like to work in London for a while".
We talked of cities and the jobs there that pay
then I said I was sorry but pressure of work ...
I couldn't stay.

He paid four francs for his coffee and slowly followed me out.
When I left him at the corner he wasn't smiling.
What could I say, it's something I know very little about?
His last words "It's hard, it's so hard" were on my mind
as we waved goodbye ..
And I left him behind.

Susan Petit - France

Poetry as a Foreign Language

"...Not really sure I'll get much out of it,
Understand what's going on,"
I whined and vacillated.
I was assured he was big
(Though not in size)
Old, blind and from the capital.
So in I went with the rest of the faculty
To the biggest hall on campus,
Packed with more than I'd ever seen before
And when the applause started from the back
And advanced with him to the front,
It was not polite or respectful
But loud and from beyond the palms of hands,
And they were standing and clapping
The old blind poet right up to the stage
With videocams and flashlights on his face
And I knew I'd not seen the likes of this before,
And not only the intoning of the country's prayers
But the readings from the campus luminaries,
Strong declamatory stuff,
Speaking to the audience. You could
Tell this because they'd clap and cheer
Right in the middle of the poet's flow.
All this told me it was not like
My home, my country,
And when the old poet began...
But why go on?

Well, yes, I told myself,
A different tradition,
An oral society, the public
Gesture, their particular
Stage of development,
The revolution, nationhood.
The excuses flooded in.
Yes, I understood in the end.
This was not British.
This was not our language at all.

Mike Ramsden - Yemen

Students

On the day it snowed in Bournemouth,
The Brazilians and Saudis went mad with delight
And rushed outside.

The Russians watched speechless from the classroom,
As Mohammed and Jesus pelted each other
With snowballs.

They ran around open mouthed and
Open armed catching snowflakes on pink
Tongues and raised palms.

Later, over a cigarette,
They talked in closed pairs, about
Their first time.

John Kay - England

Yoshiko

You told me of your friend on the other side
Of the world, attempting suicide to thwart
A lewd male boss. Suddenly stopped, face bowed.
Your eyes were tight black slots squeezing out
Teardrops, and light stung and faceted your cheeks.
Clumsily, your world cracked open, a heart
Where hot springs boiled. I thought of the Japanese
Saying on difference: "The nail that sticks out
Gets hammered down."

Vague, good daughters, you jet
Over here to be lost in study, butterflies
Sparkling over new tastes but wary of us
Whose education is an opening out.
Yoshiko, you are travelling far, your guise
Awkwardly shifting, all seismic flutters.

N. Prentice - England

Moshav

The young Irish teacher on the Moshav, got
Really friendly with the farmer. Word was
She raised more than just his language awareness, but

She worked hard, and helped talk away his
Long desert night's guard duty, dutifully listening
And collocating the opposition. She

Showed him glimpses of Ireland, lush and wet,
And green, and in return he showed her how to
Strip his M.16. In fact, by the time she left,

She was fluent. She could do it in the dark,
Faster than him, and he was impressed. But
As he said, he was only a farmer.

Afterwards, they back-chained a cigarette together, and
Smelling of gun oil and American tobacco, looked out
Into the desert, their red dots brazenly beating the stress.

John Kay - Israel

Well, I Never Fell for that Story of the Americans Landing $$$$$$

she said the) MOON in TURKEY
is more how do you say ? ? ? BEAUTIFUL
we asked but
SURELY !
it's just the = SAME = as HERE
she :-) smiled & the next day
she brought a TURKISH (moon
& hung it on the wall
it GLOWED (GLEAMED (GLARED we stared
enchanted ☺ ☺ ☺ and we got quite HOOKED
on its dancing horns

G.Griffin - Italy

Time Off Summer School, Istanbul

Sitting on the fountain in the square
watched local men
watch tourist girls
watch the mosques
in red jeans
photograph their friends

didn't buy 43 varieties of Turkish delight
lurex arm bands for belly dancers
saucepans big enough for boiling elephants
rings for toes, ears, nose, belly-button
carpet for praying,
draped over elephant saddles
or sofas
ceramic tiles with gold leaf parrots
clover leaves, scimitars,
hammer and sickles
German tourists buying wives on beaches
or buying beaches

instead caught the ferry
with commuting cleaning ladies in headscarves
paid an old man to pull my bags
on a trolley up the hill
felt guilty
helped him to push the trolley
offered to carry the heavier bag
lied about my destination
to make it shorter
tipped him money and figs
saw my father in his small bones

tourists love your names:
they come here for
names that mash like marzipan
or a hail of emperor's trumpets

it must have winters too
when the verandahs are empty on the waterfront
and the fog rides over the Golden Horn
and makes it black
when Topkapi is closed for renovations
the postcard-sellers' feet freeze sitting on the empty fountain
waiting for a pair of shorts
to follow into the mosque
used for praying

but I wouldn't believe it
any more than a cinema
stops showing pictures
or a story stops beginnings and endings
or a city stops changing its names

Jane Spiro - Turkey

Practising the Present

A man releases the locks on his café
The corrugated sheet shoots up
A dog laps water by the kerbside
The day begins

He couldn't have been more than five,
The boy riding the donkey.
Schoolgirls pass. They stop. They see
A European, tall, bearded,
Looking at the boy on the donkey.
"The boy rides a donkey," one says
with a shy glance at me
I clap softly, glad they see
What I see, glad ...
But no, they don't see
What I see, no weighing up poverty for them,
No context, no thoughts
There'll be no EFL for him today.
They run giggling
Into the simple past, their future.

Mike Ramsden - Egypt

There are Many Complications

Good morning, Professor.
Good morning. What a pleasure to see you.
I wonder if I could have a word.
Of course. I am at your entire disposal.
I just wanted to know -
We are very pleased with your teaching.
My colleague, Professor Ling,
has asked me to convey his sincere regards.
Oh, thank you. I was wondering
about the exact date of the end of term.
Indeed, yes. Dear Emily. You are so scrupulous.
How is Tony?
Yes. He's very well.
I think you told me that the end of term
was on November 14th.
Yes, yes. November 14th.
Was it not Mark Twain who said
"November is the cruellest month"?
But in the students' briefing paper
it says December 9th.
Indeed. December 9th is the agreed date.
But - excuse me if I seem dense -
I don't quite follow.
I am fighting a battle on many fronts.
Tomorrow I go to the Ministry.
I know you understand our situation.
Yes, of course.
But if the end of term is November 14th -
This is the end of the first term for the new intake.
Do you feel they have worked well?
Then perhaps I should tell the students -
Yes, please do.
Tell them that I am very pleased with their work.
It is certainly because they have such a good teacher.
About the date, Professor.
There are many complications.
Professor, I hope -
That's right, Emily. Never lose hope.
I remember, during the revolution -
As you say, Professor, there are many complications.

Michael Swan - England

Teaching Calligraphy to the Arab Prince

When the cultural attaché
had backed through the door, when
the door was shut and the polite
gestures acknowledged, when we sat
on opposite sides of the table, our notebooks
white as protocols, stiff with newness, the HBs
pointed towards each other, then
we had nothing to say so I began
with the banalities: book, pencil, table ...

repeat: book, pencil, table ...

write: book, pencil, table ...

monotonous as aping yourself in a mirror

aping yourself

in a mirror ...

I made a racket, dragging the chair
round to his side of the table. Sat
on his left, said my name, said
his name, mimed the act of writing
"In Arabic, please!"

He wrote his name in careful
curves and dots. I wrote mine
in a similar way. Right to left,
left to right, our hands
met in the middle. He grinned.

We swapped
our ways of writing and shared
a summer, smiling. I know
my name in the Koran. At court he writes
a fine Italic hand.

And the cultural attaché, against
all the odds, retained
his appointment.

G. Griffin - England

Invigilating at the Palace

Taken over is a phrase applied to palaces,
Though some might say applied to languages
As well as palaces. This one's a faculty
Of the university, leased from the Army of Redemption.
So here I am, leader for the day
In the royal *mafraj*, empty of
Cushions, carpets and leaves of *qat*,
My subjects' IDs checked, palms examined
For irregular verbs, past participles,
Aspect, the copula: all we've got
They do not have, that's why we are
A subtle race with our advanced modality,
That's why I'm here, that's why they have to
Regurgitate all we've fed them,
Their brains having to accommodate
The move from left to right.
Some say that's good, this breaking
And redirecting, like our insistence
On no "cooperation" between friends
Or clansmen; this teaches advancement
And individualism for the world of today.

The rising heat softens all endeavours.
I lapse and ruminate on the king's relatives
Who live in Tunbridge Wells. My falling head
Jerks me awake again. I read lessons in shade
Under flame-trees, banana and palm,
Then patrol between the ranks, station
Myself in a corner at the back.
Heads turn, checking whom I can see.
English had its benefits: on a shelf
I find dusty manuals on tanks and artillery,
Presents from the Soviets.

From a window I watch goats
Unloaded to feed the soldiers camping in the grounds.
Goats eat anything. They have beards
And the ghost of a smile as though
Having once known what it is to be wise.

Mike Ramsden - Yemen

Fundamental Assessment

Some place the Renaissance didn't happen
and industry of any sort is a threat
that tears from pasts that hate machines

to shelling out for GMC's.
I interview a man who loathes my life,
and cloaks his hate in language.

"The old ways are going."
They rounded sixty up last week,
slammed them up for a month or two.

The odd thing is to regret the fact,
but sympathise with tyrants
I contemn. Gun to my head,

give me the louche mob. Not
the shady bunch sure they have it right,
holier-than-thou with a fine line

in strange biros. Nothing more
corrupt than religious certainty.
Badguys are bad guys. We know the score.

So, coyish: "What old ways?"
"The architecture's different," he replies,
mocks in a polished manner.

I know he likes his lightbulbs, freezer;
returning to the sand would kill him;
the last thing he wants is a tent,

unairconditioned, without satellite.
His English excellent - we both know,
there is room for mutual deceit.

Shadowplay - no problem. We can
fence for years, me with illiberal
tolerance, he his conviction

of faith at searing noon,
and somewhere down Sharie 9,
we're distant neighbours.

In the streetsign's dust someone wrote
"street". It went by morning.
Thought and language do for us both.

By the quiet, waveless shore, he and I
share naked ground. Sand has no culture.
I wish for him to share my newish cell,

my ignorance.

Tim Cassidy - Saudi-Arabia

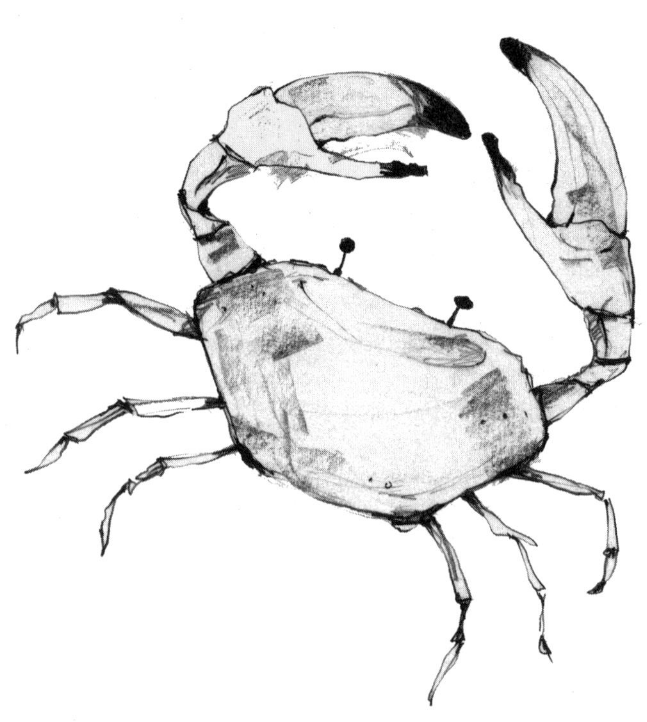

Heedless

Something I'd
never though about,
had always rushed in
careful only
of rocks and weeds and
things that nipped or bit or
caught at my toes or
slipped round in a slimy
way. You said
to pray.

Pray? Pray. Show
respect. Let
your hands not your feet
greet
the waves, give
thanks, enter the tide
like a temple. Hindu.

I always mean
to remember, to do
as you say, to pray -

I forget! Here I am.
feet first in the spray,
soaking wet, tossing
water, hugged by
invisible gods, playing
a game even older
than they.

G. Griffin - India

Ekaterina

Against the Kremlin's domes, rye-coloured, the sun sets.
    Light blue and dark blue are two different words in Russian.
    Are they two different colours, then, in "*their*" perception?
If so, the sky is changing colour. Opposite,
The White House, blacked out by the sun's fire. And we're in
    The middle, on the hunchbacked bridge, a bridge connecting
    Nothing. A bridge over no water, overarching
No road. A white-bricked folly. Chilly, I watch her lean
        Out over nothing. From her cigarette,
        Ash falls on nothing. "Don't you want one?" "*Nyet.*"

My stiff scarf love-bites me. Her eyes light up: "The first
    Russian woman who smoked was Catherine, the Empress.
    Bride of Peter the Third. She took it up to get
Off snuff. It wasn't her idea, it was the Tsar's.
He'd had enough of all the nicotine hysterics,
    Cold baths, the men at court she'd bribe to slip her snorts
    Under the tablecloth at banquets. Cigarettes,
He ruled: an altogether daintier narcotic.
        She always smoked left-handed: a Tsar's missis
        Must keep her right hand spruce for statesmen's kisses."

I kiss her left hand, face the sun. In ninety-three
    I saw that slim white tube belch soot, burnt-out and smoking,
    Not a White House in any language. And one morning
That fall, I woke to tanks exploding down the street.
This bridge was useful in the folly of brief war,
    A shield for snipers, so I heard. I can't pretend
    (Who can?) to understand the problems of this land,
Still less to know the answers. Stopping smoking, dear,
        Would be a start. Preferably while the sky
        Is light enough to give those domes their rye.

Dave Hill - Hungary

In the Dark

"I want to understand the dazzling Russian mind,"
I said, brighter than a button on a dead Tsar's suit.
"You cannot," he replied.
He burned with a mysterious Slavic incandescence.
"Let me illuminate. Here is a riddle. It is also a true story:
There is a man in the market at Yaroslavl
who sells dead lightbulbs - the filament is broken -
they have no life. But still he does business;
people buy these dead lightbulbs. Why?"
I melt in the flame of his corruscating stare
and try to blind him with my reply:
"Because they recycle the glass to make crystal sculptures?"
A superior glow spreads across his brow.
"Because Russian technologists know the strangely effulgent force
that mends the filament and brings it back to life?"
He smirks in the luminous shadows of my pyrotechnical ignorance.
"Because ..."
"I will tell you, my friend, and you will learn.
These people who buy these broken bulbs
take them to the factories where they work,
to their schools and universities, their government buildings,
and, when nobody is looking,
they unscrew the working bulbs and replace them
with the broken ones they bought in the market.
There is, of course, another part of Yaroslavl market
where they are sell the working bulbs for a higher price.
So when you ask
'How many Russian does it take to change a lightbulb?'
the answer, you will see, is not an easy one.
We are a people who cannot afford morality
yet we do have this moral:
Though there are many bright Russians,
Russia is in the dark."

Andy Archibald - Russia

Pig

"Tout se mange, sauf la merde"
It is Guillaume's first time too,
Grinning as he watches me understand
"We eat everything, except the shit."
I raise an eyebrow, aiming for nonchalance,
Knowing I will have to leave when the knife comes out.
The nine-month female squeals and wriggles
Her way to the scales guided by the farmer's hands.

"Pas si terrible" Guillaume tells me, paler,
When I poke my head back round the gate,
Gesturing a nick in his throat, striding off
To help load the pig and the bucket of blood
Into the back of his mother's car.

When I get there she is lying on two planks
In the snow, legs stiff and straight as pottery
While the butcher's blow torch colours her in
From pink to black. A block of wood jagged with bottle tops
Scrapes her expertly hairless in his circling, working hand.
He calls to Guillaume for a bucket, sloshes
The debris away. His knife slices through her belly
In the January dusk. We are an irresistible audience
The English teacher and the youngest son,
So her unpacks her for us like a showman
Her epiglottis swallowing as he flicks the tiny flap of skin.
Twanging nerves and arteries he pretends to hear a note,
Blows down the windpipe to inflate the lungs
Like a conjurer's balloon. Unravels metres of intestine
Laughing as the smell hits us, squeezing them empty
With his thumb. Heart, liver, kidneys he carries
To the kitchen, heavy on his hands, miming a stumble.

We follow him, find onions and garlic frying,
Breadcrumbs and parsley soaking in milk
Everyone hurrying for the still-warm blood.
Monique makes me Lipton's tea and asks if Guillaume fainted.
What is "boudin" in English, she wants to know,
Getting ready to trump her rival, the bank manager's wife
In class on Tuesday. "Black pudding" I say, getting warm at last,
Watching blood splash on her white linen tea towels.

Nell Farrell - France

United

Today my best student comes in with a bag she bought in Paris.
It has English writing on it.
It says: FIVE HUNDRED AND ONETH STREET.
That's what it says.
Five oh one, in figures,
and then a little "th".

I read it out loud.
She smiles: "I know, that's why I bought it.
It says something about French culture.
Trying to be English but not quite succeeding."
I think: Less true of France than of many other countries.
But I let that pass.

Still, I say it again to myself,
Quietly, while all the students chuckle,
And suddenly I hear a native speaker voice saying it.
FIVE HUNDRED AND ONETH STREET.
A native speaker who doesn't come across that particular number
every day(Who does?),
Especially in its ordinal form,
And who, in a hurry to articulate a sentence,
Goes into the default mode
That says: obey the general pattern.
That same default mode
That makes young kids say "taked"
When they've already learned "took"
Or makes full-grown adults stumble over the past of "fit" -
"The shirt fitted me?" "fit me?" "fat me?"
How natural does "Five hundred and first" sound?
Does it depend on your class, your region?
Can these things be taught?

Next week I'll buy that T-shirt I saw on sale in the market
That said "Liverpool United" in gaudy colours
("Liverpool United" - it almost works, doesn't it?)
And travel to the UK
And make a careful record
Of what percentage of people notice.

Dave Hill - Hungary

The Grey Town by the Sea

That winter of the early snowfalls,
when I took my first stumbling steps in German,
learning to read Grimms' fairytales
with a Gothic lexicon,

when even the fishing boats iced up in the Hafen,
I sat in the break between classes getting pissed
on glüwein and playing the matchstick game
neither missing England nor much missed

looking up words with my gloves on
learning to invert the frame of English syntax
I have that winter not forgotten
Husum! Theodor Sturm Stadt,

the sheer tedium of that grey town,
still oppressed by its pompous poet,
with the people who mattered away in Bonn or Berlin,
the dikes and polders flat

and featureless like the local dialect.
Then I met you two, by far the cleverest boys
in the Abitur class, angriest of your set.
What became of you, Dieter and Klaus?

We were the nazi hunters, the avenging ones.
We worked on a who's who of the local Nazis,
fingering them one by one,
stripping them of their disguises:

who had retreated from the East
leaving Prussia divided and in ruins,
who had followed Doenitz, puffy overweening Doenitz,
to surrender among these North Sea dunes.

Not the Junker who taught maths
to the fifth, soldiered all the way to Stalingrad
and back, *saw only a shuttered train near Lvov,*
nothing particularly untoward?

The forest walks with Hermerding,
his wife and gawky daughter, church
and Sunday lunch, ganz gemütlich
without alcohol: *Your work*

with the Abitur class goes quite well -
you seem quite friendly with certain boys
I'd like you to teach them Canterville.
Canterville? I was seeking other ghosts ...

Who had lost faith, who betrayed.
who had seen more than they let on
and still were silent, turning a blind eye,
tactful citizens of a forgetful nation.

Werner, the buck toothed Viennese
: *A good war, I had a good war*
in Barcelona, spying on you guys,
You don't believe me? Here ...

He rolled his sleeve up and revealed
his armpit: *My SS number, cool?*
I was no camera. That neat tattoo
pierced my detachment like a shell.

Why must I have a shit Englander in my house?
screamed Frau Edel through the walls of my room.
Why me? I was nice. I was not used
to quarrels over Lebensraum!

You burn too much wood. Think of the cost.
Learn to say sorry, be extra polite:
Sorry we won the war. Sorry you lost,
terribly sorry: *es tut mir Leid!*

It snowed and I read on: Kafka,
tragic Tucholsky in despair,
sly nazi-watcher Malaparte,
who wrote of Himmler, his buttocks bare,

being beaten with birchtwigs in the snow
by members of his bodyguard,
not so long ago, not so long ago,
before the whole show went Kaputt.

Look for evil where you find it
Curzio seemed to say, in the midst of Wonderland
or why not here in Husum?
In this grey North Sea Land,

when the smell of burning drifted over the town
only a year or two ago,
and we sniffed and looked up at the heavens
and said: we must expect snow

on Christmas Day
with the sky so laden,
and no, there was no camp for Jews,
in the whole of Schleswig Holstein, keine Juden.

Patrick Early - Germany

Leaves

Downstairs in the Kool Kanyon the kids are playing
World War Two
I even call it World War Two when it was really
the Second World War
like pitcher
Gimme the pitcher the kids say. It's like being in
a movie about the bible
Outside the leaves cover our patch of grass. Red
and yellow maple leaves
Fall was used by the English. Pitcher, fall, skillet,
World War Two
My kids are Americans now
The guy who lives next door is out with a huge
vacuum-cleaner that sucks up leaves like
candy-wrappers. His lawn looks like an army haircut.
I don't think I'll rake them. I like red and yellow.
I hear Chamberlain's voice
- From 11 o'clock this morning we shall
be at war with Nazi Germany
He's saying it very deliberately. I walk to the top
of the basement stairs and tiptoe down a few steps.
There they are, the three of them, sitting in a small
circle on folding-chairs under a green light-bulb
they've screwed into an old fixture in the ceiling. The
green light scatters over the wooden planks,
cardboard boxes, screen doors. They've made a small
space and are absolutely still. The voice stops.
Marcus gets up and puts the arm back to the beginning.
Chamberlain's creaky voice starts up again. At
11 o'clock this morning we shall be at war with
Nazi Germany
I'm sitting on the couch between my parents staring
at the dial on the Kolster-Brown. Autumn sunlight
comes through the open front door. I'm four years
old
When Chamberlain finishes Dad gets up and switches
off the wireless as though he's switching off something
really important
later an ARP man comes past on his bike, blowing a
whistle
It's a bright Sunday morning and I'm four and I
haven't even heard of America

John Daniel - England

6 APPEALS TO LANGUAGE

Words on the air ...

●●

Silent Learner

Say: I
"*I*"
Say: love
"*Love*"
Say: you
"*You*"
I love you, too. That
was a nice conversation, wasn't it.
We should relax like that and have a chat
more often.

Say: I
"*I*"
am a cat
"*Cat - but I'm not,*
I'm a dog!"
An ice-maiden dreams of herself
hot and cuddly and smelling of milk
like a fireside puppy.

"*Say: I*"
I
"*am a man*"
Man
"*dreaming my life away.*"
Dreaming the things you say,
dreaming
you understand.

James Munro - Athens

Language School, April

All over the garden, white labels. Placed
Strategically, each in a different hand,
Like tiny notices in Wonderland.
I cross one murmuring, "PATH", and then come face
To face with "TREE TRUNK" ("BARK" in brackets). There's
A bench with "BENCH" stuck to its lichened arm,
Brought into sudden contact with the name
That Eve (from Japan) and Adam (France) have just
Bestowed. Mute things, made self-proclamatory -
Wise to their nature. Best of all is one
Clinging, a little crumpled, to a twig
That frisks and jitters - clear, delicate "C"
With twelve attentive letters: "CHERRY BLOSSOM".
Brave, old words. Brash, illiterate Spring.

F.J. Dale - England

The Bright Dresses

After your *addio* - breathless, banal, the click
of the telephone, I came out into Corso Vittorio
Emmanuele. Milan's glorious main street:
rows of posh shoe shops, buckles and toecaps
on tip toe behind thick glass; at the end of the
boulevard the cathedral spires like the tails of
old seahorses: ridged, brittle and upside down;
sunlight all round me in a hot, close envelope,
with its smell of coffee and expensive brief cases;
words on the air from the English lesson I had
just been teaching: "*Sylvia never arrives late.*
Tom loves pop music and small dogs."
This is the present simple for habit. It goes on
and on I was saying. Then down the road
they came: three bright dresses in yellow, pink
and peacock blue, blurring to blobs of floating
colour inside the tears in my eyes. They jangled
the words, advanced unbearably bright towards
me: *Sylvia loves pop music. Tom never arrives*
late. Small dogs. Small dogs. Never. Loves.

Robert Seatter - Italy

It Wouldn't Do

But,
She said,
I suppose it wouldn't do
For everyone to be the same now,
Would it.

No,
I said,
There'd be less
Interesting people around,
Wouldn't there.

Fewer, interesting people,
She said,
But I suppose it wouldn't do
For everyone to speak the same now,
Would it.

John Kay - England

Souvenir of Stornoway

In Stornoway I bought the language,
Green-bound in a bookshop.

This is a telescope for seeing another world
Lived in without a second thought
As I live in my world
Where nothing happens without English verbs.

In this green language
The word for "green" is the word for "blue",
One word for "blue" is a word for "grey",
And *glas*, meaning "grey", is another word for "green".
They have ten different words for "mountain".

That world a telescope away from English
Where certain shades of green are blue
Sits on my shelf; I possess on loan
Perfect-bound ten different kinds of mountain.

Sarah Lawson - Scotland

"Und so weiter"

"Und so weiter ..." he said as she objected tearfully
to his request for divorce   the phrase meaning
his children, his mother, her mother, the American

nurse he'd leave her for. To be both German and Jew
was too much for your father, you said, exiling him
from your experience in New York neither American

nor Jew certainly not the Nazi your schoolmates
called you. Your sister, olive-skinned, black-haired
could pass in Israel you said, which you never wanted

to visit, drawn back repeatedly to the German town
your father's buried in, after his suicide in that Broadway
hotel whose windows were smeared with spring rain

when his depression began to lift   when he brought
your mother early daffodils she took as a sign of hope
their six yellow petals erect around the central tube

an open mouth, loud as a horn   then he went
to his room for his cache of pills   pocketed them
left for his private joke   signing in at the Broadway

hotel as "Hans Katzenjammer"   his energy and humour
used up he lay down to wait for what everyone said
was release   You've worn his watch for years

cyclothymic ill at ease in racist America benevolent
in teutonic phrases accent still on your tongue
you mutter at complexities "und so weiter, so weiter ..."

Dona Luongo Stein - USA

Pidgin

from *Letter to Patience*

Of course I know it isn't *you* I write
to. Is it? Elbows each side of your beer,
and chin in palms and fingers splaying bright

red nails across your cheeks as you lean near
slowly close your eyes and then as slowly
open them so that the doubt goes clear

through my own face as through the ghost of me.
"All dis tok-tok. Na dis, na dat, na dis...!
John? Enh? Wettin now? Me I no sabi!"

Then closer still, the quick touch of the kiss.
Me I no sabi, although you *do*.
A word or two of Pidgin can dismiss

all mine, can't they? Of course. Because for you
the words, most of them borrowed English though
they are, are mother tongue and come into

the breath across your tongue and lips as no
talk *full of grammah* could. I've watched them split
and writhe on the oscilloscope and know

the alterings, I am prof of it,
forgodsake, language once taught by the whips
and probably, as Bickerton has it

made up by kids who mapped the shapes of lips
to kinds of pain, and both to forms akin
to gut-known Kwa - marked now with scholarship's

circumspect star: nothing is written in
it. It is hypothetical. The play
of thought over a corpus of, yes, *sin*,

what else? There's nothing I can say.
It's true. The singer sings, the drinkers drink
their bottles empty, stand, and go away.

It's true I too deh tok, I too deh tink.
And yet, look at the photograph. You see
how words grow solid? In a child? And link

all this up into bones and blood and lovely
flesh - all this, yes, crime, from which, no sense
of it, or speaking's, going to set us free.

John Haynes - Nigeria

Proof

At last - proved right;
I'd always said
the tense was used
and then - blow me,

but yesterday,
freezing night walk
in the Old Town
with my, you know,

partner: I'd just
said "That house has
been repainted."
He replied "It's

been being re
painted now for
years." So there you
are - hard proof at
last: Present per
fect progressive
passive! Really
used.

Correct. Legit.
(Shall I forgive you for doubting it?)

(Jim Scrivener - England)

Comrades

That town we stayed in several times:
some five thousand miles from home
in a country proud to accentuate difference,
or so it felt to us; drab new flats next to bizarre
yet decorous temples, feral dogs, rich mosaics
obscured by market stalls. And that tatty place
called "*Comrades*" - at least in translation
that was what it meant, a large black pictogram
tacked on to a rusty iron plate
at the entrance to the town's only hotel.

So I learned to pronounce that native word
and practised it while travelling to villages
that pock marked the surrounding hills.
It seemed to mollify the fiercest of our guards,
and satisfy the plain-clothes men - much better
than saying "*teacher*" which had the same effect
as "*spy*". I kept that name safe on my tongue
like a boiled sweet while walking in the town,
a simple trick which gave me comfort
and softened the shock of so much uniqueness.

And when I climbed on each decrepit tour bus,
observing how the young men from the local militia
kept eyeing up the tourists as they passed,
their pudgy fingers nervous on their guns,
I'd recite that name fervently for reassurance:
Comrades, Comrades, Comrades.

David Hellens - China

The Man with the Umbrella

When I came back
I had to relearn language.
This is a lorry,
it is not a tank.
That is a paving stone,
it is not a landmine.
There is an umbrella,
it is not a rifle.
The man who is carrying the umbrella
is not going to shoot me with it.
The man who is carrying the umbrella
is not going to shoot anyone.
I have no reason to fear
the man carrying the umbrella.

And when the man puts his hand
inside his jacket
he pulls out a radio
not a hand grenade.
And when he switches the radio on
he is not detonating
a remote controlled device,
he is listening to music -
but the tune he is listening to
is the tune the militia listened to
when they machine-gunned their prisoners
against the wall I was
hiding behind.

And suddenly I see him,
I see his cruel eyes,
I see his rifle.

And I see the blood
on my own hands.

Colin Mackay - Bosnia

Caduceus

After.   Raking through
what you had said.   Banal
and yet - some phrases not
clear,   a word
ill used,   a meaning
still obscure -

of course,   for
sure!   It wasn't
one but two - meanings,
I mean - a twin string
of words,   like pearls,   like
DNA,   a double helix
looping through my brain,   two
serpents twined around
my spine,   a caduceus
of mixed intent,   a promise
to be picked up if ...

You went.   I'm left.
Trying to recall - how
did that riddle go? - which
of two to ask the way if
one tells the truth,   the other
lies and you
don't know
who
is who.

G.Griffin - Italy

Lying

When were you born?
Who is your mother?
Poor womb, if you knew who,
You would not have carried a monster

What is your race?
What is your age?
I do not have age or race
I am a servant. Everybody's servant.
Mainly for those who do not have position
For those who are looking for affection
For those who are afraid

Lying
You are the trouble maker,
To have dollars, power, poison, confidence,
To sacrifice human life

Lying
How do you permeate the whole world?
Tact and diplomacy, that is my way.
Being quick and using the lift instead of stairs
Is my principle
Moreover I am indispensable for some life in the world,
To save their life, power, their money

Lying
You are awkward. Why?
For there is another who uses the stairs

Georgette Kat Kawel - Congo

7 THE GHOST IN THE TEXTBOOK

formal abstractions, totally removed
from the actual world of real communication ...

The Cat is on the Table

Where is the cat, children?
Can't you see?
Come on, come on,
the cat is ...
the table ...
Yes, Ana, yes
the cat is on the table.
Let us all repeat:
the cat is on the table.
It is a very good sentence
for everyday conversation,
said my teacher that day.
So,
whenever you don't know what to say
in those awkward silences,
and long pauses,
whenever you start wriggling
in your seat,
and gloomy faces surround you,
This bold comment
This snappy remark
This great ice-breaker
will certainly help you.
And this is your lesson for today.

Gordana Sugden - Australia

English Lesson

I

Situational Demonstration
(proximal/distal)

This is a woman
This is a child
This is an old man
They are poor
They are hungry

They are there
We are here

Substitution Table
(The present continuous)

The women		
The children	are	walking
The old men		starving
They		

		sitting down
We	are	
		eating
		watching the television news

II

This English lesson cannot be approved.
There is no meaning in this demonstration:
formal abstractions, totally removed
from the actual world of real communication

The language taught must suit the situation,
connected with a context that makes sense.
These pointless sentences in isolation
are simply a pretence for teaching tense.

They have no worthwhile meaning to impart,
no bearing on the contexts where we know
real discourse functions in a world apart,
authentic English speakers interact.
All quite remote, as corpus studies show,
from sentences like these. And that's a fact.

Henry Widdowson - Austria

Chris

I lost Chris on the pages
of the grammar book the other night.
I never knew him.
I just wanted to know
if he had been given a dead sentence.
I let my fingers run over him only once
but then he worked well.
He might have been a carrier of mean Ing
And now I can't remember how he went.

Chris will sing for us. He had a good life.

That's how he comes to me now. Who was he?
Was he brought into the book against his will?
I reach for the table of contents, but it is crowded with strangers.
Grammatical terms, linguists,
Scattered exhibits of the body of intertwined form and meaning.
A full table with reservations.
And who am I to judge if his sentence was dead:
I'm on the outskirts, and from here
I go to crash their Indo-European party.
Twisting my tongue
I would find my way in
and ask for Chris.
They would point at the language laboratory:
"He died with foreign morphemes in his blood."
And that's when I would know:
it's not a question of dead sentences,
but of experimenting with the living ones.
He suffocated trying to form a common tongue.

Veera Rautavuoma - Finland

The English Lesson

UNIT ONE, LESSON ONE:
Is Alice making a cup of tea?
No, she isn't making a cup of tea.
Is she making a cup of coffee?
No, she isn't making a cup of coffee.
What's she doing then?

Oh flying hair, fuzz of fur, arch of sweat-back on the straw, aching-hurry, hurdle me, she cried, life is short, dance on me, put the wind up me, lust me to kingdom come, for Christ's sake take your shirt off, DON'T JUST STAND THERE!

UNIT ONE, LESSON TWO

Is Alice in the kitchen?
No, she isn't in the kitchen.
Is she in the garage?
No, she isn't in the garage.
Is she in the living-room?
No, she isn't in the living-room.
Where is she then?

In the sticky stables, smelling of wood-mould, rodents rustling under cover, slats of summer light shine lines on skin, but Alice goes for hair and shadows, the dark grunt that follows her hog pig hunger, with the ravenous cavern dilating, craving the liquid fruit, with the grasping afternoon caving in all over, under, up, between, the straw world in her mouth and still she wants much, a mountain of more ...

UNIT ONE, LESSON THREE:

Is Alice thirsty?
No, she isn't.
Is she tired?
No, she isn't.
Is she angry?
No, she isn't.
Is she hungry?
No, she isn't.
What is she then?

Lovely. Love eyes speak of dust-dancing light splicing her to him, beneath the lashes, a blur of touch, the hush of toes pried open, but whose foot is it anyway, and does it matter, and does it matter, and what matters is the moment in the moaning barn, making love cries with meaning way, oh way,

beyond

language.

Vivienne Vermes - France

Abbas is already in China

There's a note here. What does it say?
I can't read it. It is for Abbas.

But Abbas is not here. He has left us.
Perhaps it is from Mr Bates. He is here.

He has not yet left us.
But Abbas has already departed.

Who is Mr Bates? What is he?
He is a man. He says he is a writer.

Who is Abbas? I don't know.
Abbas has left us.

But this is his hat. It is the hat of Abbas.
Mr Bates is wearing it.

It is a beautiful hat
but there are holes in it.

He is glad there are holes in it.
For when the wind blows, the hat stays on his head.

Now Mr Bates has also left us.
This is Abbas. He is with Mr Bates.

Abbas and Mr Bates are talking.
What are they saying?

Now they are approaching the frontier.
Mr Bates is wearing the hat of Abbas.

Abbas is carrying the brief-case of Mr Bates.
Mr Bates is hot and Abbas is a kind man.

Now the soldier is looking at them.
What is the soldier holding? How do you know?

What are Mr Bates and Abbas doing? They are running.
Why are they running?

Now they are lying down. Perhaps they are tired.
Have they got up yet? I don't know.

Will they get up soon? Perhaps they will.
But why are you asking me these questions?

Besides, I can't see any more.
Why not?

Because my hat is too big and it covers my eyes.
Can you see through the holes in the hat?

No, I can't. The holes are too small.
And the holes are getting smaller.

Martin Bates - Sudan

From "The Spoken Arabic of Iraq"

(American Mission, Basrah - 1917)

I.

THE SHIP GOES AGAINST THE WATER

Why do you speak against me?
If you wish to learn Arabic
you must live among the Arabs.
There are soldiers all around the town.
I have two houses here, and besides these
I have four in Baghdad.

He was sitting beside me.
Who was sitting beside you?
The bridge is beyond the city.
I don't know anything about the war.
Ships cannot come here on account of the war.

I will do this for your sake.
During the night I heard the soldiers passing.
I will never learn Arabic.

II.

ANY ONE CAN LEARN ARABIC (sic)

The old house.
The good woman.
The beautiful mosque.
The broken lamp.
The hot sun.
The large earth.
The thirsty soul.

Do you know Arabic?
No, I don't know it at all.

Bring a light.
The light of the sun and the moon.
Why do you laugh?

He turned pale when he heard the news.
How many children (walad) have you?
I have four sons and three are dead.

There is much sand in the desert.
There is some bread but little water.
There is fever in Basrah.
I have fever.

The soldiers passed my house yesterday.
Get out of my way.
I saw them pass.
Leave me alone.
The time is up.
The children of Israel.
I told him to carry the child to his house.

How many churches are there in Basrah?
As many as there are mosques.

You talk like an Arab.

Edward Vanderpump - England

8 A MEETING OF LANGUAGES

The old man has waterfalls in his eyes ...

• •

Twenteen

Was the actual word you uttered
when I asked you how old you were when
you first began to learn my language,
and meaning twelve unwittingly you
coined this inestimably lovely dovetail.

And looking back now I think you yourself
when we first met a handful of years back
were a young man of that age supremely,
meaning somewhere momentarily airborne
between just twenty and the end of nineteen.

And so pure in all ways, even now,
that I could see and still can clearly
right down deep into the shining
blackness of your eyes like lit water
at the bassalia of a clean coalmine.

And glimpse there a glistening
unsullied oriental celestiana
ready to be ruthlessly lucifered
by me, or more likely by the two-faced
yen-crazed pandemonium of Japan.

But I will not, friend, let either happen
if I can help it, and I think I must help it;
for a tombird such as you, I'm sure a blue one,
comes my way rarely or the way of anyone teaching
one at such a dove-winged neap as twenteen.

Gavin Bantock - Japan

The First Men on Mercury

- We come in peace from the third planet.
Would you take us to your leader?

- Bawr stretter! Bawr. Bawr. Stretterhawl?

- This is a little plastic model
of the solar system, with working parts.
You are here and we are there and we
are now here with you, is this clear?

- Gawl horrop. Bawr. Abawrhannahanna!

- Where we come from is blue and white
with brown, you see we call the brown
here "land", the blue is "sea", and the white
is "clouds" over land and sea, we live
on the surface of the brown land,
all round is sea and clouds. We are "men".
Men come -

- Glawp men! Gawrbenner menko. Menhawl?

- Men come in peace from the third planet
which we call "earth". We are earthmen.
Take us earthmen to your leader.

- Thmen? Thmen? Bawr. Bawrhossop.
Yuleeda tan hanna. Harrabost yuleeda.

- I am the yuleeda. You see my hands,
we carry no benner, we come in peace.
The spaceways are all stretterhawn.

- Glawn peacemen all horrobhanna tantko!
Tan come at'mstrossop. Glawp yuleeda!

- Atoms are peacegawl in our harraban.
Menbat worrabost from tan hannahanna.

- You men we know bawrhossoptant. Bawr.
We know yuleeda. Go strawg backspetter quick.

- We cantantabawr, tantingko backstretter now!

- Banghapper now! Yes, third planet back.
Yuleeda will go back blue, white, brown
nowhanna! There is no more talk.

- Gawl han fasthapper?

- No. You must go back to your planet.
Go back in peace, take what you have gained
but quickly.

- Stretterworra gawl, gawl ...

- Of course, but nothing is ever the same,
now is it? You'll remember Mercury.

Edwin Morgan - Scotland

Howl

"Yam hee seens seex ti mung."
"Sixteen months?"
"Si."
"I see."

"I am?"
He blinks at me through his thick, tortoise-shell spectacles
Like an owl from a tree.
His crooked teeth have arranged themselves into a grin
But they are, like his English,
Beyond correction.

"I am? Tense?"
Homonymic irony
So lost on Alberto.

"Present perfect?" But tragic I think
More owlish blinking
And then a glimmer of something from deep within the glass.

"Haff beeng hee seens seex ti mung."
"Good! That's it."
I bite my lip, finger my lobe, hold my breath
And think of crucifixion.
Should I stop this inhumane, unhealthy humiliation?

"I've been here *since*?"
The *since* is derisive, accusatorial.
Alberto's eyes grow wider.

Since yesterday/ *Since* last week? *Since* you were born

Thudding out of me like punches

For four minutes/ *For* twelve days/ *For* sixteen months ...

A scooter buzzes past the window
I listen to it as it disappears down Calle Pilar
Heading towards the harbour.
I listen and listen
I could listen for ever.
"Ah haff beeng hee faw seex ti mung."
Albert intones at last
In a monotone to die for.

Iain Clark - Spain

I can Make myself Understood

Halloo, taxi.
Aeroport, please.
Is sunny time.
I like your urb.
Here for congress.
Academic intercourse.
Are you sposed, taximan?
I sposed, have three dwarfs.
Residual in Roma.
For my work
I insane the students.
I insane to a degree.

Michael Swan - England

"So I'm the waiter - order now."

"Use imagination - think of a food
just anything - maybe ice cream"

- *"I like ice cream"*

"I'd like"

- *"I'd like"*

"So what d'you want
... just anything, OK
.... Janos?
... Peter?

- *"Ice cream"*

"sentence?"

- *"Ice cream I like"*

"I'd like ice cream"

- *"I don't"*

Jim Scrivener - Hungary

for Rosa

"Grateful *to* you," I said,
correcting the English
of Rosa from Kazakhstan.
I then wondered if she had been right,
if the men she had helped
had been grateful *to* God *for* Rosa.

But what lifted my heart
was when she thanked me
as she got out of the car
for *lifting* her home.

Robert Chandler - London

Touch it Again, Sam

A man with a fortune must be in possession of a woman
Victorian wives were treated as divine cows
Put the oven on at an ardent heat
I felt sick and had to go to the badroom
Do you like background music while you heave lunch?
That old man has waterfalls in his eyes
The thief has got stuck in the revolting doors -
is the ambulance forthcoming?
Germany was defeated by the Alice
(Rommel was known as the Dessert Fox)
Peter Files should be locked up
Capital Punishment should not be aloud
I love to have a bath in the Mediterranean -
I do the beast stroke
If you are exhausted jump into your sofa
It's best to travel on a couch
There is a contract between Good and Evil but
Heaven exits
I love you from the button of my heart so
"Happy Birchday, Teacher"
from your Ferry Godmother.

Roger Mortimore - Spain

Does you in Russia?

Her friend was Ukrainian but spoke Russian,
But she was Russian,
Extremely Russian, extremely Muscovite in fact,
Extremely tall,
Drop-dead figure,
Eyes ice-blue like little Arctic circles of cruelty,
Hair unfairly blond, blinding.
New and rich, in her tight top.

Perfumed and painted
For a predatory evening in the bar,
Or standing close to me at the map of the world,
Where she unfortunately did not
Invite me back to her apartment
To be eaten for her dinner
Or dragged through scenes of unspeakable degradation
As her powerless sex implement,
But instead decided to give me a geography lesson:
"Here is Moscow.
And here is Siberia where not many people live
Because it's not fashionable.
I say correct?"

Demanding attention at all times,
Making me stumble over my feminine accusatives
And insisting that I correct her every mistake in English -
That high voice chiming in:
"What part of speech?
I don't understand. Explain me."

I'm sorry, Zoya.
I just can't explain you.

Dave Hill - Hungary

from **Dear My Teacher - An Errant Miscellany**

(Compiled from University Composition Assignments in Japan, 1969 to 1994)

I. Love Story

She was twenteen years old.
She was as blight as the last star of the morning.
Wearing a white blouse with long hair.

Dante - a great writer in courtly love positions.
His eyebrows are thick and bushy.
His eyes are big and bright.
He has a very big mouse.

Putting his hand on his glandfather's lap.
It became an eel and began to swim wriggly.

After a long intercourse,
during which they sometimes fell out of each other,
at last they married.

Soon she swelled by the sea.
An enormous elephant appeared.
I was lifted up by its nose.

IV. Traditional Sports

Archers should pile one big toe on another and keep silent.
I like a quiet man better than a windy man.
Take turns of one-hour shits.
The girl - she was very short-sighted - sat on my side.

I try to become a woman of culture as a social man.

V. In the Restaurant

She opened the box with her husband.
A glass of shaved ice.
John ordered the waiter.
He has died for a week.

Gavin Bantock - Japan

9 ENTER THE EXPERT

I landed there,
Islanded there, sent distantly to share
My briefcaseful of ELT ...

The Emperor's Vases

(A version of an idea found in, for example, the Sufi and the Zen traditions)

An emperor had spent all his life
completing his collection of porcelain vases.
At last he decided to write a catalogue
for scholars and succeeding generations.
So he called in a certain monk to discuss this.

"How can I describe these most precious objects
for posterity?" he asked. "This particular vase,
for example, on its gold pedestal,
which is itself a work of art.
Advise me: it seems impossible to me
to discover or even imagine its value."

"No, it's easy," replied the monk
and, stretching out his little finger,
he toppled the vase from its pedestal.

Edward Vanderpump - England

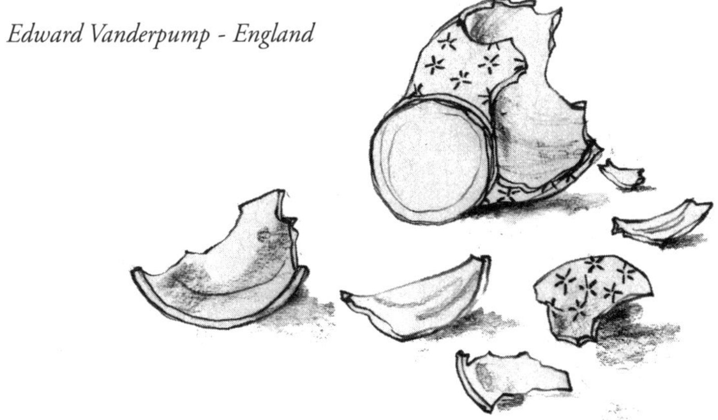

Foreign Expert

I'm an expert - it's written in the contract -
And classes sit at my feet four days a week.
Outside the classroom I revert to ignorance.
The lady selling roasted melon seeds
Has to hold up fingers for the price.
Even the obvious abacus is no good,
Although all over town everyone plays
That rectilinear rosary,
Noisy as ping-pong
On all the city's counter-tops.

Banners shout across the street
Messages to everyone but me.

Sarah Lawson - China

The Learner to the Expert

Sir, I'm "the learner" that you say you know me,
Yet I am not knowing you.
Always my name you don't use for to show me
That you are knowing me true.

You "focus" always on "the learner" - not teacher,
Not Ministry officer's action.
You make me to feel as the African creature
In zoo, just like tourist attraction.

Sir, I am hopeless to send you this greeting.
(I hope you dwell over the sea.)
But what for you say that my "needs" you are meeting
If you are not meeting me?

Gerry Abbott - England

English Language Conference in Dublin

In the morning I take the train.
Five hundred Teflers pouring into the city.
I give my hat to the cloakroom woman:
"That's a lovely hat, it suits you, and sure isn't a hat
a grand thing for keeping your head warm?"
In the conference hall a professor
with hair falling into his eyes
talks to us about teachers
indefatigably inventing tasks,
and calls for a grammar of tasks.
And then a woman in blue on how computers
are freeing us from the old stilted examples:
"My tailor is rich. My tailor is not rich."
"Shall we dance? I believe her mother is Italian."
A man with a beard urges us to teach
communicative strategies for communicative repair
as by the millenium there will be
a thousand million foreigners talking in English.
And mostly of Lower Intermediate Standard.
There is discussion on raising the status
of the non-native speaker. And on English as a vehicle
for freedom or oppression.
And on the multi-media classroom and the alternatives
to the Presentation and Practice approach.
And the day ends with Professor Bowie on Chaos:
can teaching be too orderly for its own good?
Performance is a chaos we prefer to know nothing about.
But what about learners' chaos?
"And what about teachers' chaos?"
someone mutters from the floor.
I race for the train, my mind
jumping ahead of me like a cracker,
my head a hive of bees.
"And there's a train coming in for you now this very minute,"
says the ticket collector as he punches the ticket.
In the train I remember
I've forgotten my hat.

Olivia McMahon - Scotland

Visiting Expert

Dropping at night
Into a city braceleted with light
And, with day dawning, queuing stiff and yawning

I felt the pull
Of suntime on my body, like the full
Moon's on the seas or on the mind's unease.

I felt the suck
Of clothing on my back; I heard the cluck
Of tuneful tongues; the hot air hurt my lungs.

I landed there,
Islanded there, sent distantly to share
My briefcaseful of ELT. Disgraceful,

For what they learned
From me I wouldn't care to say. I earned
My fee, no doubt; they mildly heard me out,

Produced a scatter
Of questions germane to another matter,
Gave thanks and praise and went their gentle ways.

Out in the street
Dead dogs like bagpipes bellied at their feet.
Beside the road their gilded temples glowed.

But then what they
Taught me was golden. It is hard to say,
For what's absurd's expressing it in words;

Their expertise
Could not be typed up (double-spaced) to please
An academic journal or External.

But when through cloud
I dropped back on a city screaming loud
"Borrow!", "Spend!" and "Buy!" I knew that I

(Though they'd not told
Me this) had learned a bit about the gold
Found in the earth; how little the stuff's worth.

Gerry Abbott - Burma

He Knows Words

He is a very verbal person.
He knows words.
They spiral from his mouth,
float, interlace,
drift to the carpet.

His mouth *is* words.
He chews his food with
thirty-two gleaming synonyms,
digests it with
ten yards of speaking tubes,
does not so much talk crap as
crap talk.
Adjectives, verbs and nouns
clothe his bones,
his skeleton is syntactically perfect,
he does not suffer from
dangling participles, or
split infinitives;
through his veins flows
purest rhetoric;
he is jointed with conjunctions;
at the sides of his head
in place of ears, are
two parentheses.

He came close and touched me,
it was as if a dictionary reached for me.
He kissed me, and
my mouth was full
of the dry taste of adverbs.
He put a proposition to me
erected a grammatical structure
ejaculated a fountain of
most exquisite semantics.

His linguistic features enclose two lacunae
barred windows, where
terrified eyes
will continue to peer
till he comes to the end of his sentence:
the final
full stop.

Michael Swan - England

The Post-modern Lecture

Dr Martin Lindsey Minelli laconically muses on modernity
He is precise and roundabout,
He is bony and sparse,
He is milk-made:
His hair, his eyebrows, his eyelashes are as milky as milk;
He is wrapped in milk paper
And his mouth spurts out sentences like an udder.
They splash on the table, spread out, then gather in puddles.
Long tongues lusting after theory
Lap them up but the words spurt so fast,
The puddles become a pool, the pool a lake.
The audience take to boats and bob up and down on a foam of phrases,
Scooping up curdled words from the deep with buckets.

There are more names than words:
Names upon names:
Foucault and Fiedler,
Kristeva, Kuhn and Klinkowitz,
Barthes, Baudrillard, Britten and Bhabha;
Bhabha is the most beloved of Dr Minelli's names -
Who is this Bhabha?
Ali Baba of the thieves or Babar the Elephant Bhabha?

My boat has sprung a leak, torpedoed by a sharp quotation;
I try to bail out the coagulating names but they stick in my bucket;
I sink in a language bog, gulping.
The words are rancid in my mouth,
They take me in.

Jeremy Jacobson - Romania

Meditation in a Lecture on Pragmatics

May your glass of water
transmute
to sulphuric acid.

May your little spectacles
spontaneously combust.

May your trousers fall down
revealing
improbably erotic underwear.

May bats fly out of your mouth
in search of nourishment.

May your hidden lusts
appear in graphic form
on the screen behind you.

May the lectern grow feet
and scuttle away.

May the OHP
take you by the throat
and shake you
till your dry balls rattle.

May the microphone
modulate your drone
add guitar backing
boost the bass to maximum
and feed it
at 200 decibels
up your backside.

May the audience turn to vultures
hop onto the stage
and rend you
with great curved beaks.

And (in conclusion)
may your unmarked grave
disappear for ever
buried
in the blessedly silent sands.

Michael Swan - England

The Visiting Linguist

He was judged by the old university to be
A man about whom nothing bad could be said
And all of his colleagues were certain that he
Knew enough about words to deserve a degree
To prove he had so much there in his head.

Mainstream written discourses were people-like, he said
Moving on to what he thought you should dream about in bed
About metastructure content gloss and positive evaluation
About semantics and pragmatics and of course reformulation

He'd categorised and analysed and split open bits of words
He'd even written articles on the cries of starving Kurds
He knew about transitives and ergatives and goals
But he never really understood why *The Sun* had used "coal-holes"

He'd never been across the yard to fill the scuttle up
Or hidden in the coal-hole among the lovely muck
And imagined that the Germans were knocking at the door
And shivered there all morning, hiding from the gore

So he couldn't know the coal-hole hid a million childhood schemes
He was too busy with his lexis and his dogma and his rhemes
Too busy with the many words that buzzed inside his head
To notice that his audience had either nodded off or fled.

Len Webster - England

The Visiting Author

From Cairo to Jakarta and Caracas
his fame goes with him as an author
of English Language Text Books.
He brings help in easy explanations,
dispenses rules like mottoes in a Christmas cracker,
leads only where the way is clear,
asks only questions that can be answered.
In these rich lands he is as simple as the T shirts
in washed-out colours he packs before departure:
pressed and folded,
the sleeves turned deftly upon themselves,
they lie in piles, neat as his explanations:
the difference between *I make money*
and *I am making money.*

Olivia McMahon: Scotland

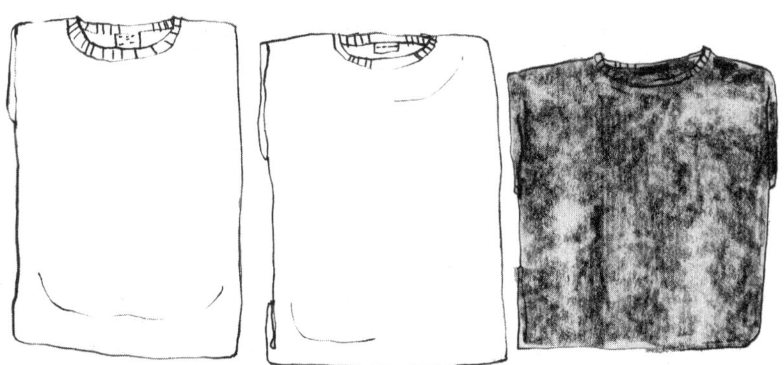

The Broken Glasses

I remember a summer in Alexandria
when the Dean of Inspectors had broken his glasses.
He peered through one lens
the other stuffed with cotton wool
at me at sea on my new course
while my head still tangled with the old one
between the Blue and the White Nile
and the competitors were galloping ahead
on horseback among the pyramids
the reins between their smoky teeth.

The Dean of Inspectors had broken his glasses
and my voice was pinking with fear
as he peered at my muddled manuscript.
Words and chairs creaked through the Cecil Hotel.
The editor had hired the conference room
and underlined my uncertainty
with his razor-edged moustache.

The sunset glowed on the Dean's cotton wool
but of my sorry manuscript
he could make neither head nor tail.
He needed more than the seven types of ambiguity
he had studied at Sheffield.

We had only one lens between us
so an explosion in the square outside
among the screaming taxis
passed almost unnoticed.

Martin Bates - Egypt

10 MIGRATION AND EXILE

Where in your papers does it say
that your face belongs to you ...?

Home tuition, 1980

"Coe" she said, locking the door,
defeated by the final consonants,
while I shooed away the strays.

On Thursdays we usually play lotto
and they try to say "trousers"
and ply me with rice.

Last week we role played shoe shops
and they giggled at the sizes
and held out an open purse.

But today three year old Duong
strafes the hospital waiting room,
revealing the slit in his pants

and San Sao stares at the green wall
blank as the South China Sea
where, dry-mouthed, dry-eyed

she watched her husband slide
the dead baby over the side
and shivered as the boat of wailing

carried her, small, unresisting,
anxious to please, to this world
where she can't say cold.

Carole Bromley - England

Exile

Where in your papers does it say
that your face belongs to you?
Did you get a stamp
for that shadow
I always see behind you?
What made you think
you could come alone?

Is it a friend
gone without a word
or the lover you left?
What happened to
the child who used to stand
next to you at the bus stop?

When you crossed the mountains
headlights picked out figures
from the rocks of unknown passes:
heads, hands, known and vanished.
Seashines spelt lost names
as the aircraft lifted
into a sky called grief.

That severing from ground
is one death
and your ghost trails
its old selves
resisting alien light.

Here there's no word for
sky or friend or lover
and the air only makes
dark mirages of those
who loved or tortured you.

Like the horse's head
blotted on the floss of stars,
the flame of your dead friends
shapes you now.

And now I see your face
so far, so safe
do you know I never look at you
without seeing that you haven't come alone?

Jane McLaughlin - England

The Round Pond, Kensington Gardens

"70p for deckchair, please."
I looked up. Oriental eyes.
Thin wispy beard. Hair to the shoulders.
Cheeks chived with acne.
He stood with grace and apology;
his eyes plumbed mine, cast and plumbed,
seemed to find their depth,
smiled at a recognition.
He sat beside me.

"In Japan, people like herd of ducks;
if little bit different,
squawked and pecked away.
Banish! Ostracise!
Here I swim the pond
happy as a charm.
In Japan gays hide light under bushel,
peep out once in while.
My father Salaryman.
Brother Salaryman. Whole roost!

"I go different way,
search for Shin Jodo, Pure Land,
slowly tread Eightfold Path.
Zen prophet Bodhidarma
stare at wall for nine years,
suddenly see satori.
I study pond, learn waves.
Pond my star and compass
will lead me to my prayer.
But many steps to take,
many ways to splash."

A week or two later
I went back to the pond,
strolled round the deckchairs.
The ticketman was blond,
the accent Australian;
"It was the Parks Police.
Here at midnight.
The case was coming to court.
One night he got a deckie,
faced it to the pond,
wound his ticket box round his neck,
wound it round and round."

Nick Blair - England

St Mary's Allotments

Walking Rashid home we pass
rough, graffitied walls screaming:

VERMIN GO HOME, YOU BIN WARNED

Nearby, allotments with staked beans,
Medusa-like lettuce.
Opposite, infants skip
on tarmac playgrounds with
Koala bear rucksacks.

"Miss, in Mogadishu, I am shoot two man."
Almost infantile hands try to obscure the pain.
"Speaking English, yes Miss, but writing, no writing, no."

Susan Willock - England

The Jail in North Bohemia

My heart is wandering
About my body
Just now it stopped
And up in the throat
It's beating

I wish it would come back
To where it's at home
And I could feel free not alone
Amidst the jail of smog

My heart is beating
Up on my tongue
What shall we do
To free our children
And
My son
MY SON!

Hana Masopustová - Czech Republic

The Social Security Office

"It's only my Dad who came from Jamaica,"
he says, his hands and head a-trembling now,
"And I'm from Lancashire, a British Passport."
"Yes, of course," I say, and see his swarthy,
gentle face with twitching eyes and frightened gaze.
"I need to smoke, you know. I asked her,
that one, blonde, behind the grille.
She screamed at me, and asked me,
'Is it stressful if you do not get your cash?'
Oh yes, I suffer from depression,
need to see my son. My mum,
she's Scottish, yes, I've got the papers here."
He clutches at my wrist, and nearby leaning
on the dirty window of Minerva Street,
his friend says "How do you spell 'health'?
I've got to fill this form, no pen is here,
no paper in the toilet either." Sign of man's
inhumanity to man, humiliation of the poor.
"It's 'h-e-ll' isn't it?" He asks.
And yes, I think, that's how it's spelled today.
Two yellow snapdragons from Clydeside pavements
I push into their tatty, smelly jacket pockets.
"It's luck", he says, and laughs again,
a Caribbean calypso in his eyes.

Janine Fitzpatrick - Scotland

Camouflage

from *Letter to Patience*

A myth of hope. A camouflage. The call
of hoopoes came out of his lips. The stream
was him, so was the tick and tocking fall

of rain. He was the leaves, the inner seam
of sun and chlorophyll from which his eye
evolved, his variation on a theme.

Someone had seen him in the market buy-
ing fish. Someone had seen him in the taxi
park, holding a bag, sunshades, tie-dye

boot slamming, shouting touts, the dust. A tree,
a rag, a blackboard in the village. *Loot,*
spell it, spell *loot,* spell *looter,* feel them, see

the shape of them, the words, the rhymes, spell *shoot,*
like gizo-gizo making loops unreal
out of his body. Write it: *rifle, boot,*

relocation. What else? It's you, the real.
It comes of saying of it out. You *are,*
it is, they're doing this, say it, they steal,

the dam makers, Barclays: com - pra -
dor. *Write it down.* His shadow slips between
our chair backs in a mud-walled township bar

Or *is* it his? The girl's thighs gently seem
to swell under the table next to him.
She holds his simple blood. She holds the stream,

the leaves and twigs like camouflage denim,
the chlorophyll, the Ancestors who call
out jokes across a brilliance where they swim....

John Haynes - Nigeria

11 THE SECOND PERSON

half way round the world, the two of us
weighed up from the many we've both known ...

I'm just a Little Girl

It won't be easy
to forget those eyes
which took me off
from land to stars.
Those beautiful blue eyes
blue like the sky
in the middle of the sunny day;
blue like the ocean
when the waves finish their game.

It won't be easy,
but that's the way it is,
our magic stopped
'cause we are just kids.
And every time when I close my eyes
I see you walking through my mind.

So, if you, my favourite friend
ever read these lines I needed to send
you'll know I love you even more,
but don't forget:
I'm just a little girl.

Bojana Milošević - Yugoslavia

Little Room in Kyushu

"... and makes one little room an everywhere." John Donne

Perhaps neither of us thought anything
special about the other that spring day
you came in spluttering flu, jetlagged
from your trek, fifteen hours and five miles high,
passing over the pole to that small berge.

It was clear you'd find your way round soon
without looking for assistance or advice.
Though you say you never really flirted,
as the last train left, I own it was you
who raised your parted lips to kiss,

and after that, you had to stay the night.
You were full of innocent strategy
and coy protest, and my flat was nothing:
bedroom, kitchen, loo and one big space
I'd wait for dust to pile in before I hoovered.

Mine took two days, and when my plane touched down
amidst a blitz of signs and narrow roads,
we seized the first hotel that came in sight.
I still couldn't see why it was different
from anywhere else I'd ever been,

till we came to your parents' apartment
and I saw your cell, each square foot fitted
with a watchmaker's precision. You take
a measuring tape wherever you go.
Your cupboards finely cram the season's clothes,

I struggle, kick like an overweight birth
in some small womb, get by but wonder
how I ever came to live with your family,
the grandmother from whom we hide the truth,
the aunt who's been a hostess in a bar,

most of all that bright azimuth
history planned that brought me flying
half way round the world, the two of us
weighed up from the many we've both known,
to bijou, bliss out here in your box-room.

Your split ends shed all over the place,
to find and scotch them are my smaller joys.
Your stereo's the smallest on the earth,
like your telly, which hides all we do. Please,
turn it up. Extend our walls of noise.

Tim Cassidy - Japan

Lost for Words

Alessandra, honeyed by the twilight,
recited verse from Michelangelo.
I didn't understand a word, although
she stunned me with her eyes, as if I might.
"What does it mean?" I asked.

With a delightfully sly smile she said,
"You still don't know?
Is difficult in English. I speak slow.
'*L'intensa voglia* '. So! Is simple. Right?"

She leaned towards me, folding back the book,
breathing above my shoulder as she traced
each word, and brushed her palm against my hand.

Her tawny hair, her laugh, her sidelong look.
"*L'intensa voglia*". Fingers interlaced,
the words grew easier to understand.

Paul Cowlan - Germany

Two Loves

Coming upon two pictures of Nadia
(Who? Nadia. Nadie. Nothing.
Nobody. Vanished into the past.)
I found two long hairs,
dark against the printed page,
and thought them pressed, like brittle flowers,
as her old keepsakes too.

I held them to the light.
No olive sheen, not raven black,
but wiry, reddish gold
(English summer-blonde):
my daughter's fair surprise
between the pages of the Shakespeare quotes,
"When in disgrace with fortune and men's eyes."

Edward Vanderpump - England

A Lesson in Love

I love you transitively,
but you, the object of my love,
are loved but passively.

Maybe in the simple past
you loved me too,
and if (impossible condition!)
I'd loved you less, you'd love me still.

But third conditionals cannot be.
I've lost your love and hope to find
the present perfect as they claim
or futures where we'll love again.

Caroline Treitel - England

Silent Words

I seek words
in the deep well of my mind
to tell you
what I feel
in your own tongue.

The bucket goes down,
tied up to a knotted rope.
It meets gushing words,
gurgling words,
clear and quiet lakes,
rivers overflowing
towards an immense sea
of tempests.

I can't find words
to describe
my trepid emotions:
subtle nuances,
impalpable differences,
like transparent shadows
against the light.

Too many doubts,
I fear to make mistakes,
to be misunderstood,
to break the spell
of this newborn love.

Unaware,
you smile brightly at me,
your face comes closer
to mine
and springs, lakes,
rivers of words
meet silently
on our lips.

Luciana Spatoloni - Italy

Out of Class Activities

After classes, in the quiet college buffet,
We fixed a time that she should come whilst drinking coke.
My English student, final year, she said she wanted
To learn Italian: I'd mentioned living there
Two years to illustrate the difference between
Simple past and present perfect in class that day.
It was, of course, public pretence on both our parts.
She was twenty-eight and knew just what she wanted,
Although it was a very risky game for her,
Good small-town girl, well-known family. And me, too.
Once there, alone inside my tiny one-roomed flat,
She made it very clear that she was keen to learn.
She said: "I am a tailor," peeling off her dress,
"I make my clothes myself at home." I was impressed.
This recurred many times during the next few weeks,
Whilst we practised the third conditionals in class:
"What will/would happen if ... ?" "What would have happened if ... ?"
I moved away - new job, got married, grew a beard
And visiting the town again for "auld lang syne"
I met her on the street by chance, two kids in tow.
Examining my hirsute face she conjured up:
"Your bear is well." I could do little but agree,
But later wondered where those past times disappear:
Things perfect, conditional, and the way with words.

David A. Hill - Kosovo

Foreign

Make love to me in Serbo-Croat
But handle me with care
Touch my body in far off places
Run your fingers through my hair

Kiss me up in French
Then whisper Finnish down my ear
And blow across my Spanish face
To dry away this olive tear

Sing me Balkan love songs
Or Scottish ballads from the border
Dance with me in Georgian hills
Like a Slav or Bulgar

Talk to me in Basque or Welsh
Tuscan, Celt or Sami
Smother me in dialogue
Make it all sound Greek to me

Say "I love you" with every tongue you speak
Then tell me that you love me
Comfort me in foreign parts
Enrapture me completely

Christopher Hadfield - Czech Republic

English for Domestic Purposes

I remember you showing me the flat
And the bathroom, the two fresh towels
For my personal use: one for "upstairs",
One for "downstairs". Travelling through
From the orange harvest near Sparta,
I was welcome for the week at least.

Thirteen years on, I have reached home.

I can say this now - our little secret
As long as you lived: once I asked
What had woken me, roused beneath
A light Greek sheet. "Guess!" you said,
"I was kissing Mr An*th*ony Good Day; rise
And shine" - Anthony being my middle name,

But not in the language lab of our love.

Laurence James - Greece

For Louis J..., Killed in a Car Crash

Louis wrote
in an English test
that when he got married
he would like a house
easy for his wife
without upstairs
with the floor built with stones
outside the town
with a big garden
because he liked dogs
and to have a happy dog
you need a garden
also because generally
wives like flowers.
But perhaps, he wrote
in conclusion,
it will be only
a beautiful dream.

Michael Swan - England

Words in his Pocket

"*Can one say...?*" I used to ask before your lesson.
You stood by the window with a mug of tea,
allowing the life of the street to surf over all
you knew and had to teach.
Looking at you, I realised from the silent
passioning in your face that anything
was possible. In your own good time
you turned. "*Yes, you can say it that way.*"

We were your audience. Your body lit, and lonely.
On an underground train I jostled with new phrases
while you in a slow voice
demonstrated to the next class
what a long way English tenses could go.
Quoted Shakespeare to students
still struggling with idiomatic terms
"*All words have heads and tails.*"

St James' Park. I shouldered my bag.
Astonished that in a sun-splashed café
people were using the prepositions you'd taught.
Years later, at the same spot, I learned of your death.
Tulips in a vase curved into opposite directions.
"*Yes, one can put it that way,*" I overheard a passer-by.
At that moment, the way forward
seemed like the way back.

Christine McNeill - England

In Memory of Tshijik Charnelle

For her who was
lifted up to heaven
taken by the speed of the car.

In trousers, she was
hardly recognised as a girl.
For her who was
The wood, ancient black wood
Sunny, from her childhood

An error of human judgement
An accident in a busy road
A peaceful boy face down

For her who lives among angels
Who sings, praises Tshinawej, God our Father,
And pray for her parents, brother and sister

Death, you had taken her roughly
In sounds of a bang, a deforestation,
Falling down, killing the small tree
The first tree in a forest
Her family protests

Red image of head and frozen body
Whose memory still is
A drift from understanding.

Georgette Kat Kawel - Congo

12 EXPATRIATE LIFE

But the truth was we'd been in another country,
and disaffected from our own, found some brief solace
when some found harsher, brittle lives back home ...

Doing Donne

(Suzhou University, Spring semester)

I know these are umbrellas, but for today
They are a compass, or pair of compasses,
As Donne says. See how I hold them at the top:
When one leg moves, the other leans the same
Direction. Donne is one leg, the lady is the other.
"Conceit" we call this; Donne the master poet
Used these metaphors, extended to
The breaking point, "like gold to airy thin-
Ness beat".

The umbrellas - compasses, I mean -
Are joined, even though the bottom ends
Are far apart. So the poet's soul
Is one with the lady's soul - joined
You see, in spite of all appearances.

And I am running this far perimeter
Myself, still joined by letters and the odd
Phone call. I've better postal service than
John Donne, but then I've travelled farther than
He could have done. When I have done, then I
Will leave my Donne behind, as that is what
Is done by foreign teachers here, the done
Thing, as Jack himself would say.

Remember this example of conceit,
A metaphysical conceit. It may
Well be a question in the midterm test.

Sarah Lawson - China

Expatriate

Somewhere between the sea and the dark blue devil
my grin combines the contented smile of a man entirely
successful in a nine-house hamlet on an island
in the Inland Sea, and the faded snarl of a willing exile.

I sit in a rotting rattan rocking chair playing with
words like that in steaming inertia and nursing
the brown music of the spheres in the expanding
paunch of my universe. I've discovered perspiration
and chopped onions have the same smell,
like me, somehow intensely likeable.

Middle-age, it seems, is a lazy touch-and-go race between
the windblown charisma of a white mane and absolute
sunblazed baldness, ending in a draw: one perfectly groomed
grey hair. Mirrors tell me better than vernacular newspapers
all I need to know about the changing face of the world.

My wooden house is like a museum in a provincial town
nobody visits: full of working clocks, British souvenirs,
used pewter ashtrays, dragons, statues of heathen gods;
a mildewed ship loaded with textbooks permanently out of print.

I swim in the beautiful black waters of my students' eyes:
it is my business to excite them with the glamorous
calibres of language, and to teach them how to say
Good morning ten thousand times without me or them
once sounding tired, and with perfect intonation.

People here repeatedly ask me the difference between
words like *maybe* and *perhaps*, and I can't answer,
possibly because we probably never really understand
the language we speak. And when I visit England,
people on trains think I come from Russia, so often in fact
that I imagine I really was born somewhere beyond
Samarkand. But it's more liberating to walk, irresponsibly
alien, through my village birthplace in the Midland hills.

I feel now like a kind of kingpin in a foreign court,
but a soothsaying friend once told me I would die
falling ablaze from a great height. I'm extra
careful when I travel by air, but there's so little
a man can do. My strongest hope is that whenever
it's going to happen, not too many people will be hurt
in the huge earthquake I'm convinced will occur
a few days before my outlandish funeral.

Gavin Bantock - Japan

Sequence of Tenses

If this is the Balkans, I may after all appreciate
cool disagreements; politeness in the shop queue;
no politics or religion; handkerchieves; after you; -
my home-town hypocrisy is easy on my palate.

If you don't pay attention, you'll never learn
the nine million acceptable ways of avoiding
getting involved - learning them, you'll find, is something
for which English will supremely serve your turn.

If the government allowed opposition, people surely would
feel that they had a stake in the system.
That's what happens in Dumfries and Birmingham.
Why should you let politics cause bad blood?

If I write this on the blackboard, people look away -
"All animals are equal, but some are more equal than others."
"Each man kills the things he loves." "We happy band of brothers."
That's just English literature. Whatever did I say?

If the old man died tomorrow, it wouldn't make
any difference. Everything's sorted out - the wheels
will turn smoothly as before. The international community feels
no-one would risk chaos for some old feud's sake.

If they'd listened to us, say the wise men, all this
could have been avoided. We warned against the passions
and greed of trouble-makers and local politicians.
Did they listen to us? O no - and now look at the mess!

If it were up to you, you wouldn't be here
in this impossible, beautiful place, after so many
centuries of impossible, ugly deeds, when there aren't any
ways of stopping it being just this year.

If I had my choice again, would I still say, "I don't mind
Sarajevo - why not?" I've helped give every side's top men
maximum exposure - millions have got involved! Then
it was true as now - we have to take as we find.

Stephen Meyer - Bosnia

Evacuation

The wind gathers up
An Arabian winter
On the peninsula
And there's talk of war.

Morning is a noise
Of demented crows
Imitating ducks.
The anthem floats into my home
From school assembly up the hill.
Then the students limber up:
Wahed itneen telata arbaa

I wonder what I can let go.
I stick old photos in albums
After twenty years,
Read letters, those who've died,
The number begins to grow alarmingly.
I think about insurance
And put a price upon my life.

When it comes down to it,
When the trouble starts,
I'll be burdened with my files
            Ego scriptum scripsi
No clothes, no stereo, no computer.
I begin to fill a box:
Cuttings from newspapers,
Bus tickets, plane tickets,
Menus, poems to the nth attempt,
All the rejects too, novels, stories,
Then weigh things in the balance,
Whether I'll be back or not,
Whether to be done with it and pack the lot,
What I'll put in the final case.

Mike Ramsden - Yemen

Dispersals

"I want to be buried at home, in ________ "
he heard someone say - at which the thought
started like a surprised hare of what
he wanted, since most likely he'd die
far from wherever "home" was. No sense
in it perhaps, the wish seeming to presuppose
a place of "rest" and an awareness of "resting",
both questionable. Still, imagine it ... "laid
to rest". To become a false coherence, in death
one of the locals? Better as ashes, dispersed
as he already was: a pinch here and there
like seasoning, in that river, on that hill.

Donald Adamson - Scotland

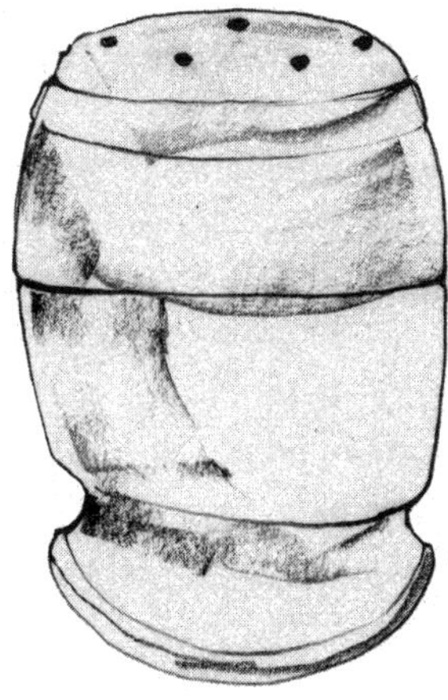

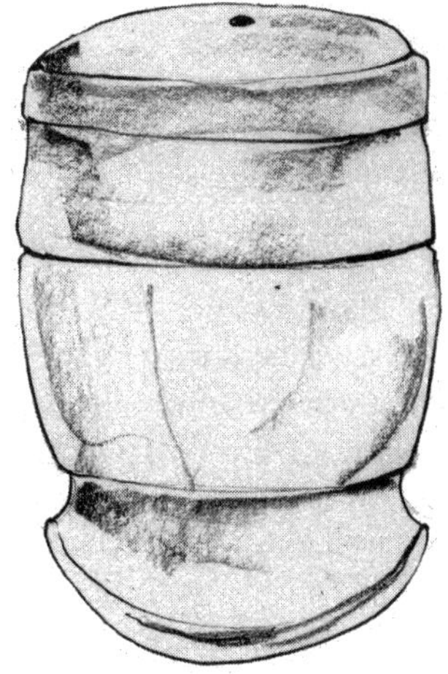

Janice's Spanish Album

Janice had the language down. She'd never asked me
round before, but I was one of the few left from two years
whom she had known. We laughed at times we'd soon

call old and good, and she offered to show me more
which she had kept in a brown, leather-bound album.
We saw the recent past and joked at pulled faces,

expressions shocked by light, clownish-costumed friends
forever youthful in the flash, red-eyed with drink
or wrong aperture, whom time would never change

or daunt with pain. Two years were in her hands,
as if in aspic in her album with clear-plastic leaves
that trapped the air and froze us in their creases.

We leafed back further to a time before I came
to the southern province, and she put faces to
names I'd only heard of, jokers and recluses,

lovers, travellers, professionals, the plain weird.
Further still, till it seemed the faces looked the same:
mine was there with those she'd known twelve years before,

skinny-dipping in the hills, taking jugs of wine
and loves to pools by mint-lined shores no longer secret,
but shared among each wave who came and went.

I thought of all the tedious partings she had wept.
I'd thought our wave was different, unlike those who'd been.
But the truth was we'd been in another country,

and disaffected from our own, found some brief solace
when some found harsher, brittle lives back home.
I still didn't know there's more to this: it happens

any place one goes. Friends are yours a while, then go.
Stay and it's a passing show. I needn't have left.
I see all I'd have known wherever I'd been.

Tim Cassidy - Spain

13 LANGUAGE PLAY

Whenever was the past simple ... ?

Time Past, Time Present, Time ...

(A Reflection)

Whenever was the past simple?
Looking back when I left, I knew
We had had some good times
In the past, perfect early days.
Since leaving I have enjoyed
A year without stress -
Could this be deemed a present perfect?
Yet at present I am uneasy -
Not sleeping participally well,
Trying to cope with the future
With no intentions, no fixed plans,
Without the will for immediate decisions -
No certainties for even one year hence.
I am, you could say - tense.

Camille Flaherty - England

Animal Crackers

It was raining cats and dogs as I hoofed it up the stairs to his office, but I was more aware of the butterflies in my stomach and the large frog in my throat, when I met that wolf in sheep's clothing and trotted out my C.V.

I gritted my teeth as he glared at me and almost wished I had not sought new pastures, aiming to spread my wings and wanting to be a high flier. But I also knew that I had to take the bull by the horns with the bit between the teeth, if I were ever to become a fat cat or even a cool one and get a buzz out of life.

So I tried to worm things out of him, buttering him up and lionising him without falling at the first fence. But that snake in the grass could smell a rat a mile off and wouldn't play ball or take the bait or even talk turkey.

Having clawed his way to the top, he was now cock a hoop about being top dog and didn't want any wise owls prowling about and carping at his methods. Nor did he want anyone swanning around his holy of holies, creaming off his best ideas. He would do all the crowing himself, thank you!

I wasn't ready to chicken out so soon, so I rabbited on about possible birds of a feather, but he just remained dog in the manger and I could see that I was barking up the wrong tree, if I ever imagined he would let me get a foot in the door. I suppose I always knew that the leopard does not change its spots.

So I threw in the towel, saying that it was all water off a duck's back to me and that his office was not even large enough to swing a cat in and that, anyway, I only did interviews for kicks and had never really intended to get involved in all this monkey business.

I tried not to look too sheepish as I slunk down the stairs, my tail between my legs, and out into the dusk. People were milling about in the rush hour and being herded into the tube. It was still raining cats and dogs and I decided then and there that I'd had enough of the rat race and living in the fast lane - I would choose the quiet life from now on.

Rosemary Keith - England

The Idiomatic English Teacher

(or Keeping Body and Soul Together)

To You, Who ...

Often do not turn a hair
When replying off the top of your head,
Which should be screwed on the right way.
Often you are up to your eyes in work,
And need eyes in the back of your head.
You also need to keep your nose clean,
As well as keeping it to the grindstone.
Your ears are often burning,
Having kept one of them to the ground.
You often play it by ear,
And have to turn the other cheek.
That was said with tongue in cheek!
You often live from hand to mouth,
And need to keep your chin up.
Sometimes you have to stick your neck out,
And may even become a pain in the neck!
You should not get a chip on your shoulder,
But must keep abreast of the times.
Usually your heart is in the right place,
And you have no stomach for infighting.
Sometimes you have to chance your arm -
More power to your elbow!
Frequently you have your hands full,
And may become all fingers and thumbs.
But somehow you keep your finger on the pulse.
At bottom you are dedicated,
And often on your last legs.
Revive! Students think you are the bees' knees!
Fortunately you have your feet firmly on the ground.
Occasionally you have to dig your heels in,
And even put your foot down.
A pity you sometimes put your foot in it!
At times you have to toe the line,
Even though you may tread on somebody's toes.
All in all, you are a teacher, from top to toe.

R.R. Jordan - England

The Alphabet

Letters make words.
Words make phrases.
Phrases make paragraphs.
Paragraphs make compositions.
Compositions make books.
Books tell us
very important things.
Every letter
means or appears to mean something.
A is the first, the director.
B is the servant of the leader.
C is a loadstone.
D is a semicircle.
E is a fork without a handle.
F is a television aerial.
G is a dangerous curve.
H is a rugby goalpost.
I is a straight line.
J is a hook.
K is one line with victory on its side.
L is a corner.
M is like two mountains.
N is Zorro asleep.
O is a circle.
P is a flag.
Q is a circle with one foot.
R is a "P" with a lame leg.
S is the sign of Superman.
T is a telegraph pole.
U is a loadstone on its side.
V is the sign of peace.
W is a double victory.
X marks the place.
Y is an aerial on Mars.
Z is the sign of Zorro.

Eduardo González Chillón - Spain

A Little Nightmare for Students of English

1. Enough is Enough

He had been very thorough
working his way through
the malt whiskies at "The Plough"
but now he sat outside in the rain, soaked through
and racked with a hacking cough.
He struggled to his feet, although
far from steady, and tottered off with a loud hiccough.

2. A Little Run Down

Jake was a little run down
when his wife ordered him to put out the cat,
and consequently he fell out with her.
Grumpily he put out the light and fell into bed
and into a restless sleep,
dreaming of his native border fells
and those fell and haunted forests
being destroyed by the ruthless tree fellers.

He awoke with a start
and started to get up,
but felt so giddy and run down,
he woke his wife and asked her to run
downstairs and phone the doctor.
His nose was running,
he was running a temperature,
and he'd got "the runs".

It wasn't only *his* luck that was running out,
for his doctor, while running over from the surgery,
had run over his cat,
swerved into the chicken run,
whereon the birds had run amuck,
out onto the main road, causing a run of accidents.
He was run in by the police,
who discovered his insurance had run out.

So much for his chance of running for mayor!
And now he'd run up a massive bill.
The batteries of his mobile phone had run down,
so he couldn't phone the surgery.
By the time he reached Jake, he'd run out of patience,
"gone round the bend", "run off the rails".
He drew a lancet from his bag and ran him through,
watching unmoved as his patient's blood ran free.

Nigel Cameron - England

Le Rose et le Rouge

There is a young boy who loves pink
Which is a good colour, I think.
    But in marking his story
    I'm awfully sorry
To add to his pink this red ink.

Learics

1

There was an old man on some rocks
Who offered a lady some chocs.
    He promised her love,
    And all heaven above -
As long as she mended his socks.

2

There was an old person of Ealing
Watching the wallpaper peeling.
    Fearing the trap
    Of a wallpaper wrap
He decided to sleep on the ceiling.

Edigne Schaller - Germany

from **Stressing the Importance of English**

... But hardly do I begin to teach
this language quite beyond my reach
when I begin to see its power
that makes me struggle by the hour!
No sooner do I learn to spell
than I begin to feel her spell!
One spelling with different meanings!
The same sound but different spellings!

If you lead then you're not led;
but with lead in you, you could be dead!
Read a book till it is read,
even if your eyes go red!
And if you're reading about Reading,
you'll know just what I keep on dreading!

"Object of" and "object to"
might seem simple enough to you.
But I'm simply left entranced
at the entrance! Have never advanced!
And although I can't her charms refuse,
will all my efforts remain refuse?!

Yes, I've always feared the most
that awesome, fearful, "stressful" ghost:
while you may think you're *important*,
a slip of stress, and you're *impotent*!

HS Sandhu - India

Warra Cheek!

If there's one thing that gets right up my nose
It's students giving scores on what teacher knows
How dare they rate me second class
I'd like to know where they find the brass
Writing down they think I'm weak
I wonder where they get the cheek
If they keep saying my grammar's queer
I'll give it to them till it comes out of their ear
That'll teach them to mind their betters
When I'm teaching these clouts their letters
Saying English expressions are too much hassle
Well they go down very well up in Newcastle
So there's nothing wrong with Geordie slang
An' if they divent stop it I'm gannin yem!

Warra = What a
Divent = don't
ganning = going
yem = home

Susan Petit - France

Englyn and other Words

I like new words that come from
other places like the past
like englyn jonquin
termagant and cad
words to eat with noodles
wear with matching hats
or buy tickets for
that pop up like cacti
or unfold like plastic macs

I enjoy words which are not yet
things
in the way that suburbs rhubarb
teeth and drains
are things

words with are still
spicey savoury
rude and bad
to dip in the soup
like englyn jonquin
termagant and cad

Jane Spiro - England

Fishers at dawn
catch
reflected images
in soul-nets ...

Haiku Gone Wrong

Everything is a story
night time a song.

Fishers at dawn
catch
reflected images
in soul-nets.

Father was right.
It wasn't worth trying.

Borivoje Baltezarevic - Scotland

Waves and Sand

Waves are licking the sand
Gently with charm
It's an honour
To be close to them
To taste delight of their hands
To be as one
Just for a second
But it's an innocence
It's a wild glow
Could it be a sin
To be touched by them?
It can't be
God left it forever
With no change
For eternity

Anna Panowicz - Poland

Thief in the Dream

Where was I? Oh yes, the thief entered the dream ...
... and I woke up, The wind was blowing so strong that it seemed the sea.
I dreamed it was the sea! I must say, I must say
I felt it was the sea! In no way ... without way
But how could it be?!! It is hard to say.

Once I heard a bird but did not listen to him
Once I saw a star but did not know it was not that
but the echo of something bright
Glancing at the road
I was entering a storm.

Where was I? Oh yes, the thief entered the dream

Then I heard my laugh - again my laugh -
and really felt the joy, oh what a joy!
Again I've dreamed the sea!
But how could it be?!!
Because there was no thief in the dream!

So I tried to sleep ... I was so tired, so tired
... It was getting dark then
when the dream came to its end
The wind blew again ...

The thief entered the dream
there was no thief in the dream
but a dream in the thief.

Esli González López - Mexico

Seasons

Autumn is yellow,
spring and summer are bright.
And I am winter,
so I am white.

Cathy Kokushkina - Bulgaria

Four Seasons

Asama mountain,
in your winter kimono
you are meekly chaste.

Ravenous is the
mind of a hermit; the mist
satiates his thoughts.

The red sun settles
over Saku's bosom - it's
taken for granted.

Russet autumn leaves
amass on the velvet ground
in genuflection.

Valerian Plavan - Japan

English in Autumn

Wind is blowing
My English words are coming
Leaves are falling down
and my mind is getting on
paper down.

Ingrida Pikturnienė- Lithuania

"I am a Syllable"

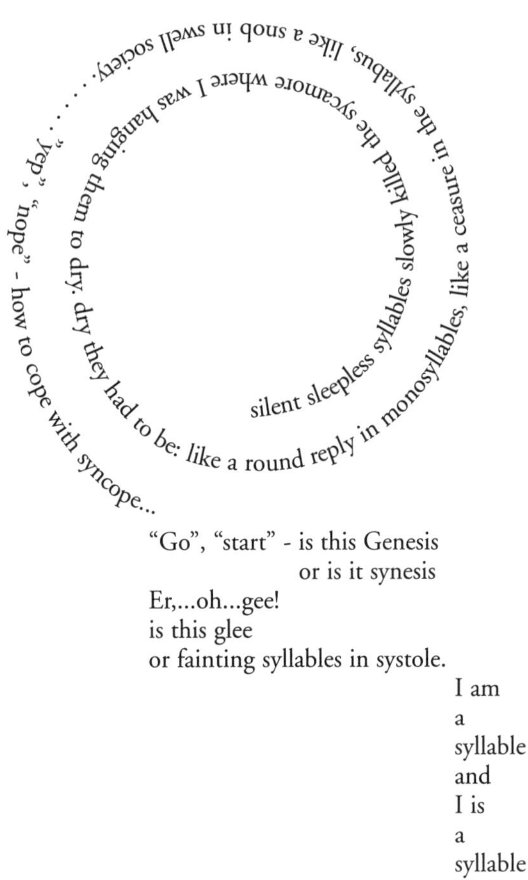

"Go", "start" - is this Genesis
or is it synesis
Er,...oh...gee!
is this glee
or fainting syllables in systole.

I am
a
syllable
and
I is
a
syllable
Ha!

Rositza Alexandrova - Bulgaria

Sometimes

People murmur things
With apple blossom
In their ears,
Not knowing that the wolf
Is howling along the corridor
(With cigars breathing
The Earthly sweat,
Drained and photograph
eD).

Once

I saw a crow
staring at me:
I drew a wave rolling in the backyard
as it flew away,
torn to pieces
smashed against
my weedless heart.
salt with sweat in it,
forgotten inside a chalk box.
Ghosts can sing as well
as you, I was told,
and yet, photographs tell no lies.
Buy, thus, a wordless foreign legend
and dwell on it with lust,
stone upon stone.
bullets circling around a name.
After, maybe you can step in
to the Island I had long
forgotten.
                How to dance?

Natividade de Figueiredo Lemos - Portugal

A Smile

I do not understand why people love you
You are too serious, not easy to keep out,
A smile, that is enough

People will put you in the Sahara, or Jupiter,
Yet they will be surprised by the number
Of friends.

Who are you?
That is simple, easy, a smile
I am part of a human being's expression
The expression of feeling, rejoicing, suffering.
My poison can chain up multitudes in my
kingdom

Do not be afraid, I am not the Lion
I am the one who takes away lovers from one
Shore to another

Life can be Calvary without me
Indeed I can soften the angry face
I create anew a world for unloved children,
Homeless
I soothe the muddled spirit
I am a diamond hidden in sand
I am the star in the night
A radiant star on your face brothers and sisters

Please, please do not put me indoors,
Let me live, radiate on your face.
A smile

Georgette Kat Kawel - Congo

Notes on the poems

• Note that some poems, especially those in Section 8, contain "errors" which produce a humorous or poetic effect. Speakers of other languages should be careful when using them as models for writing! Some poems contain words and collocations invented by the learner which are technically incorrect but which have an effect strangely suggestive of poetic creativity.

• Conversely, many native-speakers writing poems in English vary the rules for poetic effect; e.g. articles are sometimes omitted; punctuation marks may also be omitted; line endings may serve instead of commas etc to mark breaks.

Page 13 Other Languages - uses figuratively several terms from linguistics and phonetics.

Page 23 A New World - Rift Valley - in Kenya; see also author's biographic details.

Page 25 Opening a Window - 1974 - contains grammar mistakes used to surreal effect; A Man for all seasons - play by Robert Bolt about the trial of Sir Thomas More.

Page 27 Doing "Used to" ... - Twiggy: an English model famous in the '60's; Haram - forbidden or unlawful (Arabic).

Page 29 Always More to Learn - contains "learner language" with comic mistakes and slang; fogging - similar to a popular obscenity; kernackered - knackered = very tired (slang).

Page 42 May Poem - first frosts - in the southern hemisphere, of course, May is at the onset of winter.

Page 44 In Munich - alles für meinen Kindern = everything for my children (German); el niño - a hurricane that recently devastated parts of America.

Page 47 The Language Missionaries - Daniel Jones - English phonetician who devised the phonetic alphabet; RP - Received Pronunciation - standardised form on which Jones' alphabet was based - associated with "posh" accent of southern England, as in heowm for home.; home counties - region round London; schwa = "weak" sound of unstressed vowels in English.

Page 48 *How to Say "Night, Night"* - civil service - administrative wing of government; privy council - advisers to the monarch and more recently elected government; cloth of gold - ceremonial cloth associated with monarchs, heralds etc; lingua franca - language for communication between speakers of different languages.

Page 53 *Moshav* - strip his M.16 - take apart his machine-gun for cleaning; Moshav - type of settlement in Israel.

Page 58 *Invigilating at the Palace* - mafraj - top floor of Yemeni house for receiving guests; qat - green leaves chewed as a stimulant; IDs - identity documents; aspect, copula, modality - grammatical terms; Tunbridge Wells - town in Kent favoured by well-off retired people.

Page 59 *Fundamental Assessment* - about an interview with a fundamentalist; sharie - street.

Page 62 *Ekaterina* - nyet = no (Russian); snorts = doses of a drug (slang); ninety-three = attempted coup against Gorbachev's reforming government in 1993; rye - a grain for bread and kind of whisky, light brown in colour.

Page 63 *How many ... does it take to change a light bulb?* - usually a joke at the expense of people thought to be stupid;which proves to be not the case here.

Page 65 *United* - Go into default mode = follow the normal procedure (in machines)

Page 66 *The Grey Town by the Sea* is Husum in Schleswig-Holstein, birthplace of nineteenth century nationalist writer Theodor Sturm; Hafen = harbour; glüwein = a mulled wine drink; Abitur = school-leaving exam; Doenitz = Nazi Admiral appointed Führer at Hitler's death; Junker = Prussian military aristocrat; shuttered train - train taking Jews and other prisoners to Death Camps; ganz gemütlich = nice and cosy; Canterville - Oscar Wilde's story Canterville's Ghost; Lebensraum = "living space" - slogan used by Nazis to justify territorial aggression; es tut mir Leid = I am very sorry; Tucholsky - social democrat journalist driven into exile and suicide by the Nazis; (Curzio) Malaparte - Italian fascist author of Kaputt, describing disenchantment with the Nazis from the inside; keine Juden = no Jews.

Page 69 *Leaves* - was written in Minnesota; the author reflects on differences between US and British usage: pitcher- jug; skillet - frying-pan; fall - autumn; World War Two - Second World War.

Page 71 *The Bright Dresses* - addio = goodbye (Italian).

Page 72 *It wouldn't do* - less/fewer - a favourite grammatical distinction with EFL teachers.

Page 72 *Souvenir of Stornoway* - Stornoway is a town in the Hebrides, north-west Scotland, where the ancient Gaelic language is spoken.

Page 73 *Und so weiter* = and so on (German); Hans Katsenjammer - from a comic strip called "The Katsenjammer Kids".

Page 74 *Pidgin* - "All dis tok-tok ... Me I no sabi!" - "All this talking , first this, then that, then this. John, eh, what's the matter? I don't understand." Grammah - standard English; Kwa - family of west African languages, including Yoruba.

Page 75 *Proof* - present perfect progressive passive - a form more common in grammar books than in life.

Page 78 *Caduceus* - symbol of the messenger god Mercury/Hermes, a winged rod with 2 snakes twined round it in opposite directions, symbolising the harmonious conjunction of opposites; similar in shape to the double helix form of DNA chains which carry genes.

Page 79 *Lying* - "I want to express the idea that lying can take the place of people who can't be heard. This is what is happening every day all over the world." (GKK)

Page 81 *English Lesson* - corpus studies - analyses of actual spoken and written texts.

Page 82 *Chris* - Indo-European - large family of languages including many spoken in Europe and Asia; Finnish belongs to a different group of languages; morphemes - minimal bits of words carrying meaning.

Page 84 *Abbas is already in China* - inspired by a telex message seen in an office in Khartoum; the hat with holes was bought in Memphis and given to the Counsellor for English at the Egyptian Ministry of Education; the rest is mythical.

Page 91 *I can Make myself Understood* - contains several punning deliberate mistakes.

Page 104 *The Broken Glasses* - Seven Types of Ambiguity - famous book by poet and critic William Empson, who taught at Sheffield University where the Dean of Inspectors at the Egyptian Ministry of Education - Dr Girgis Rashidi - obtained his doctorate.

Page 106 *Exile* - horse's head - the Horsehead is a dark nebula in the constellation Orion, so called because of its shape.

Page 107 *The Round Pond* ... Kensington Gardens - large park in West London; Hide light under bushel - conceal one's talents or abilities;roost - perch where birds congregate; deckie - deckchair (Australian slang); the poem also contains examples of learner (Japanese) English.

Page 110 Camouflage - gizo-gizo -spider, trickster in folk-tales (Hausa)

Page 112 Little Room in Kyushu - azimuth - astronomical term for arc in the sky; split ends - loose hairs with split ends.

Page 113 Lost for Words - l'intensa voglia = powerful desire (Italian).

Page 114 Two Loves - nadie = nobody (Spanish); quotation from Shakespeare - last line of Sonnet 29.

Page 118 English for Domestic Purposes - the *t* with silent *h* in Anthony might by a learner be mispronounced *th*.

Page 120 In Memory of Tshijik Charnelle - she was the author's niece - "a lovely, beautiful girl". Tshinawej = God, in Rwund, a language spoken in Congo.

Page 121 Doing Donne - contains references to poems by John (or Jack) Donne: Valediction Forbidding Mourning, which uses the drawing compass as symbol of attachment surviving separation; Hymn to God the Father - where the poet puns on his own name sounding the same as the word done.

Page 124 Evacuation - wahed itneen telata arba - one, two, three, four (Arabic); ego scriptum scripsi - I wrote the script (Latin)

Page 132 Learics - the title comes from the name of the nineteenth century nonsense poet who wrote Limericks - Edward Lear.

Page 134 Warra Cheek! - Geordie - dialect of north-eastern England around Newcastle.

Page 140 A Smile - "something which doesn't cost much but does a lot in human life ... a bit the expression of myself. The smile makes things easy." (GKK)

Typology of Poems

These lists are intended to help you navigate your way round the poems. Their aim is to guide your reading and also to encourage creative writing. They may give you ideas for developing your own writing in similar ways, using the poems as models for inspiration. To find the page reference for a poem, please see the Index of Titles.

Themes and settings

Learning

These poems give expression to the **experience of learning** - inner feelings: hope and possibility; struggle: obstacle and difficulty, fear, risk, isolation; excitement, pleasure & achievement; looking around us - the effects of environment.

Many are written by learners and some by children. As a learner, some of the poems may prompt you to write about your own experience in a similar way; or in a different way - expressing different feelings, or from the point of view of another - parent, teacher etc. Change a poem by a learner to show how the teacher sees it, or vice versa.

- **poems expressing the learner's point of view:**

  Trip without End
  About Getting the Exact Word in English
  In a Small English Room
  Linguistic Clock
  No Walls
  The Learner to the Expert
  The White Room
  Words

- **looking around us - poetic use of the setting:**

  English in Autumn
  ESOL
  Roofs
  The White Room
  "Thuh"

• **as seen by the teacher:**

A New World
Poetry Hour
A Special Case
Roofs

• **classroom interaction:** the hurly-burly of classroom activities and exchanges, planned and unexpected, interruptions, control - different voices:

A Poetry Hour
Always More to Learn
Doing "Used to": A Bad Day at the Chalk-Face
English Lesson
Helen
Opening a Window - 1974
"So I'm the Waiter - Order Now."
"Thuh"

• **the teacher being observed**

Always More to Learn
The Importance of Socks
Wolves

• **teachers reflect on their role, the subject and the process:**

As teacher, as learner
ESOL
Fundamental Assessment
Invigilating at the Palace
Lesson
Professional Deformation
Renewing my Contract
Teaching English for Special Purposes
Visiting Expert

• **"experts" - varieties of knowledge - ignorance - practising & preaching**

English Language Conference in Dublin
Foreign Expert

The Emperor's Vases
The Learner to the Expert
The Visiting Author
The Visiting Expert
Visiting Expert

• **attitudes to poetry:**

Doing Donne
Poetry as a Foreign Language
Poetry Hour

Language

Thinking and feeling about language - what it looks and sounds like, what it can do or fail to do. Many of these poems are from the point of view of the teacher; some might be used as counter-models - to write about how the learner feels. Language rouses strong feelings; it is a link between the personal and the public, the local and the universal, at the root of understanding and misunderstanding. Through writing, learners can explore what the new language means to them: does it offer freedom or bind them? How does it affect their relations with their own culture and traditions? Teachers may also find this a fertile field: what is it I am teaching?

The process of learning and attempting to communicate can generate interesting poetry. The learner's language or "interlanguage" may offer strangely poetic utterances. The constricted, sometimes sterile language of the textbook can spark off poetry when placed beside real-life situations and feelings.

Finally, some poems are written for learning - to help memorise actual language features such as idioms and phrasal verbs. They offer opportunities for light-hearted play with the foreign language.

• **language and the self** - identity, ownership, memory, personal history, development:

In Munich
May Poem
Pidgin
You, & Me
"Und so weiter"

• **the strangeness and appeal of other languages:**

Other Languages
Slug
Souvenir of Stornoway
The Grey Town by the Sea
The Language Missionaries
Translating German

• **language as focus for feeling or thought** - where words take on heightened importance between people; words as images:

"Und so weiter"
English for Domestic Purposes
Expatriate
He Knows Words
Home Tuition, 1980
It wouldn't Do
Language School, April
Lost for Words
Out of Class Activities
Pidgin
Professional Deformation
Rosie
Silent Learner
The Bright Dresses
Words in his Pocket

• **language in its social or historical context:**

Comrades
Ekaterina
Evacuation
Fundamental Assessment
Heedless
How to say "night night"
Invigilating at the Palace
No Walls
Philology
Speaking with English
In the Dark
The Grey Town by the Sea
The Language Missionaries
The Man with the Umbrella
Warra Cheek!

• **echoes of TEFL** - in tension with real life

A Lesson in Love
Abbas is already in China
Chris
Doing "Used to": A Bad Day at the Chalk-Face
English Lesson
From "The Spoken Arabic of Iraq"
Opening a Window - 1974
Out of Class Activities
Practising the Present
Teaching Calligraphy to the Arab Prince
The Bright Dresses
The Cat is on the Table
The English Lesson
The Man with an Umbrella

• **use of TEFL devices:**

drill - *Doing "Used to"...*
Opening a Window
The English Lesson

role play - *"So I'm the Waiter - Order Now"*
substitution table - *English Lesson*

• **communication:** understanding and misunderstanding, getting through and not getting through:

Always more to Learn
Caduceus
Howl
I can Make myself Understood
"So I'm the Waiter - Order now."
There are many Complications

• **poetic effects of "error", learner language, mixing of languages:**

Always More to Learn
Dear My Teacher ...
Does you in Russia?
First Men on Mercury
for Rosa

Howl
I can Make myself Understood
It wouldn't Do
Out of Class Activities
St Mary's Allotments
The Learner to the Expert
The Round Pond, Kensington Gardens
Touch it again, Sam
Twenteen
United

- **Language play - for learning purposes:**

idioms and fixed metaphors:

A Little Nightmare for Students of English
Animal Crackers
The Idiomatic English Teacher

spelling

Stressing the Importance of English

Interpersonal writing

These poems arise from working or personal relationships. They express one-to-one feelings using the public language. Again, they may be used as models for your own writing, perhaps by reversing the point of view. They offer opportunities for developing one's own personal relations with the foreign language.

the teacher addressing the student

Does you in Russia?
for Rosa
Fundamental Assessment
Lesson
Renewing my Contract
Teaching Calligraphy
The Coffee Bar
Twenteen

- **student addressing teacher**

Words in his Pocket

- **poems showing empathy, imagining what it's like to be the other**

  As teacher, as learner
  Howl
  Lesson
  Lessons: 1973-1998
  Renewing my Contract
  The Social Security Office
  Twenteen
  Words in his Pocket
  Yoshiko

- **love and intimate feeling:**

  Caduceus
  Does you in Russia?
  English for Domestic Purposes
  From the Institute of Universal History
  I'm just a Little Girl
  It wouldn't Do
  Little Room in Kyushu
  Lost for Words
  Moshav
  Out of Class Activities
  Pidgin
  Silent Learner
  Silent Words
  The Bright Dresses
  The English Lesson
  Time Past, Time Present, Time ...
  Two Loves
  You, & Me

- **elegy & loss, lament:**

  Deep
  For Louis J..., Killed in a Car Crash
  In Memory of Tshijik Charnelle
  The Jail in North Bohemia
  Words in his Pocket

The cultural setting

Both teachers and learners are engaged in an adventure which may combine excitement and fear: exposure of teachers to different environments causing them to look anew at their own culture and assumptions about people and life; exposure of students to the whole setting of the language - contemporary and sometimes historical. It is not just the language that we teach/learn. Both teaching and learning are often done in conditions of exile, uprooting from one's past, loneliness and isolation. Many learners will empathise with the feelings expressed in these poems and may wish to express their own feelings in their own voice.

See also the list above: **language in its social or historical context.**

• **exil**e - isolation, loneliness, exclusion, separation, uprooting, the shock of migration:

the refugee

Always More to Learn
Exile
Home Tuition, 1980
Lessons: 1973-1998
Opening a Window, 1974
St Mary's Allotments

the outsider

Camouflage
Renewing my Contract
The Round Pond, Kensington Gardens
Yoshiko
You, & Me

poverty and exclusion:

English Lesson
Practising the Present
The Coffee Bar

the immigrant

A New World
Lesson
The Social Security Office

the expatriate

Doing Donne
Evacuation
Expatriate
Janice's Spanish Album

- **cultural interchange** -strangeness of other cultures & places, difference, comparison:

A New World
Always More to Learn
Comrades
Ekaterina
Little Room in Kyushu
Pig
Poetry as a Foreign Language
Students
The Answer is not an Easy one
Yoshiko

Poetic features displayed by the poems

This list, which is not exhaustive, is a guide to selecting the poems for reading and for using as models for writing, to develop one's creative communication skills or to have fun with words.

- **humour**

A Little Nightmare for Students of English
A Poetry Hour
Abbas is already in China
Always more to Learn
Brain Waves
Dear my Teacher ...
Doing "Used to": A Bad Day at the Chalk-Face
Doing Donne
English Language Conference in Dublin
First Men on Mercury
Helen
Howl
I can Make myself Understood
Professional Deformation
Animal Crackers

"So I'm the Waiter - Order now."
Sound Barrier
Students
The English Lesson
The Idiomatic English Teacher
There are many Complications
Touch it again, Sam
Warra Cheek!
Well, I never Fell for that Story ...

- **word-play** (punning):

A Lesson in Love
Doing Donne
Time Past, Time Present, Time ...

- **irony**

Invigilating at the Palace
It wouldn't Do
Opening a Window - 1974
The Cat is on the Table
The English Lesson
The Importance of Socks
There are many Complications
To Travel

- **satire & invective:**

He Knows Words
Meditation in a Lecture on Pragmatics
The Post-Modern Lecture
The Visiting Author
The Visiting Expert

- **pathos**

English Lesson
For Louis J..., Killed in a Car Crash
Home Tuition, 1980
Opening a Window - 1974
St Mary's Allotments
The Jail in North Bohemia

The Round Pond, Kensington Gardens
The Social Security Office
Yoshiko

• poems notable for their **imagery**: metaphor and analogy - what is ... like? word-pictures

A Smile
A Trip without End
About Getting the Exact Word in English
Caduceus
Camouflage
English & I
ESOL
Exile
For Seasons
Haiku Gone Wrong
He Knows Words
Learning English
Lying
Meditation in a Lecture on Pragmatics
New Shoes
Once
Other languages
Seasons
Silent Words
Slug
Sometimes
The English Lesson
The Jail in North Bohemia
The Post-Modern Lecture
Thief in the Dream
Transfiguration
Translating German
Twenteen
Waves and Sand
Wolves

- **riddles and mysteries:**

  "I am a Syllable"
  A Smile
  Chris
  Lying
  Once
  Sometimes
  The Alphabet
  Thief in the Dream

- **patterns of sound and shape**

  "*I am a Syllable*": concrete poetry
  A Poetry Hour - ballad form + rhyme
  Brain Waves: rhyme - short line ending stanza
  Camouflage: rhyme, syllabics (3 line stanzas, 10-syllable lines)
  Foreign: ballad form
  Haiku Gone Wrong:haiku (gone wrong)
  Le Rose et le Rouge/Learics: limericks
  Lessons: 1973-1998: villanelle
  Other languages: alliteration
  Philology: ballad form, rhyme
  Sound Barrier : rhyme - ballad stanza- alliteration
  Stressing the Importance of English: rhyme
  Visiting Expert: internal rhyme, patterning with line-length

- **dialogue poems:**

  Abbas is already in China
  Speaking with English
  There are many Complications
  Helen

- poem as tapestry of **quotations:**

  To my Beloved E.L...

Notes on Contributers to the Anthology

Abbott, Gerry (*Visiting Expert, The Learner to the Expert*) - spent half his professional life in Asia and Africa' has published 3 books on Burma, his last overseas posting; now based in Manchester; co-author with Bob Jordan of *English all over the Place.*

Adamson, Donald (*Dispersals*) - one of the competition judges; Scottish poet and EFL materials-writer; currently lecturing (creative writing) at Jyväskylä University, Finland; winner of the *Herald* "Millenium Poem" and other competitions; his collection *Clearer Water*, published by Wider Eye Publications, Kirkudbright, Scotland

Alexandrova, Rositza (*Speaking with English,"I am a Syllable"*) - a secondary school pupil at the Foreign Languages School, Haskovo, Bulgaria

Archibald, Andy (*In the Dark*) - secondary school teacher in London and student of phonetics; previously taught in Japan in USA; published in mainstream poetry magazines

Baltezarevic, Borivoje (*Linguistic Clock, Haiku Gone Wrong*) - from Nis in Yugoslavia, student at Edinburgh University IALS 1998-9; interested in literature since early childhood; "my initiation into poetry was through the poems of Rabindranath Tagore and Khalil Gibran".

Bantock, Gavin (T*wenteen, Dear my Teacher, Expatriate*) - widely published poet who has lived for 30 years in Japan, where he teaches literature and directs plays; his poem *Expatriate* won third prize in the Arvon International Poetry Competition, 1998.

Bates, Martin (*Abbas is already in China, The Broken Glasses*) - has taught in Argentina, Sudan, Iran and Egypt; written materials for ESP and middle eastern secondary schools; published 4 collections of poetry.

Berry, Roger Stephen (*Sound Barrier*) - Associate Professor, Lingnan University, Hong Kong; formerly taught EFL in Hungary, Poland, China; has published two books on grammar.

Bjorkman, Elizabeth & David, Franke (*New Shoes*) - students at EFL Hastings, Sussex.

Blair, Nick (*The Round Pond, Kensington Gardens*) - is based in London.

Bromley, Carole (*Home Tuition, 1980*) - runner-up in the competition; teaches English in York to students of many nationalities; some have accompanied her on

Arvon courses, including a Bosnian refugee who wrote her first drafts in Serbo-Croat; poems published in magazines and competition anthologies - her poem was inspired by working with recently arrived Vietnamese boat people.

Cameron, Nigel (*A Little Nightmare for Students of English*) - artist, sculptor and ex-architect living in Devon; winner of the Exeter Riddles Prize.

Cassidy, Tim (*Fundamental Assessment, Janice's Spanish Album, Little Room in Kyushu, Teaching English for Special Purposes*) - has taught EFL in various countries; now based in Saudi-Arabia; published poetry in leading UK magazines.

Chandler, Robert (*for Rosa*) - is based in London.

Clark, Iain (Howl) - from Edinburgh, he has taught EFL in Spain and now lectures in communication at Fife College

Cowlan, Paul F (*Lost for Words*) - an English acoustic rock performer/songwriter living in Frankfurt, Germany; he has published poetry in leading magazines and anthologies; 1998 was a good year for him: winner of Tabla Poetry Competition; runner-up, Stand Poetry Competition; entry in Daily Telegraph/Arvon "ring of words" anthology.

Dale, FJ (*Language School, April*) - lives in Blossom Street, Cambridge; her poem was inspired by a garden in Saffron Walden.

Daniel, John (Leaves) - one of the competition judges; has taught literature in Britain and the USA; painter and poet, he recently won the Exeter Poetry Competition; his poem was written while he was living in Minnesota.

Dubé, Janet (*How to say "Night Night"*) - a Londoner who has lived in Wales for 25 years; two of her grandparents were a Cockney butler and a Welsh-speaking cook; her daughter taught EFL in Spain and brought back a Catalan boy-friend who was fascinated by the expression "night night",

Early, Patrick (*The Language Missionaries,The Grey Town by the Sea*) - has worked in many countries with the British Council and was Representative in Sudan, Yugoslavia and Brazil; currently directing a charitable organisation for Moldovan orphans, and writing and publishing poetry.

Farrell, Nell (*Pig*) - from Nottinghamshire, now working in social work training in Sheffield; taught English in France using Roger McGough's poems and Joni Mitchell's lyrics; she "fell so deeply in love with things French that she now supports Arsenal".

Fitzpatrick, Janine (The Social Security Office) - based in Glasgow; widely published poet, prose-writer, journalist, translator; translated Brecht for Bavarian radio; performing poetry with music of James Macmillan, Glasgow University, 1999; composed prayer-poem for Labour Party Conference, 1999.

Flaherty, Camille (*Time Past, Time Present, Time...*) - from Bristol, after studying Russian and French, she took up health education and TEFL: "more a performer/reader than writer/poet"; at present working on a scheme to initiate EFL students in the language of Shakespeare.

González Chillón, Eduardo (*The Alphabet*) - is a student at the British Institute for Young Learners, Madrid.

González López, Esli (*Thief in a Dream*) - a Mexican student at Anglo World Cambridge, 1998; according to her teacher, Peter Hannan, her poem followed her parting with fellow-students and looking at a bright star in the night sky over Kings College, Cambridge.

Griffin, G (*Caduceus, Heedless, Teaching Calligraphy to an Arab Prince, Well, I never Fell for that Story of the Americans Landing*) - has taught EFL and calligraphy in London, Rome and Barcelona; worked in media and communication in Italy; now lives "on an antique island on an Italian lake, writing the island's story and local folklore. And poetry."

Hadfield, Charles (*Always more to Learn*) - has taught in China, Madagascar, India; now in Devon; publishes poems combined with visual images; recent collections published by University of Salzburg.

Hadfield, Christopher (*Foreign*) - teaches at the University of West Bohemia, Plzen, Czech Republic.

Harris, Edjane (*No Walls, Travel*) - born Edjane Batista Miranda in Bahia, Brazil, she now lives in Senegal, where she paints and teaches dance, Spanish and English.

Haynes, John (*Camouflage, Pidgin, "Thuh"*) - won second prize in the competition; taught many years at Ahmadu Bello University, Nigeria; now in Hampshire, working on a book-length poem - *Letter to Patience* - from which *Pidgin* and *Camouflage* are taken; a longer selection in an anthology due from Enitharmon, 2000; also written books of literary criticism - on African Poetry and on Style.

Hellens, David (*Comrades*) - is based in Brighton.

Hill, Dave (*Does you in Russia?, Ekaterina, Philology,United*) - has taught in many countries and now works in Hungary.

Hill, David A (*Out of Class Activities, Professional Deformation*) - ELT consultant and materials-writer based in Budapest, Hungary; previously taught in Britain, Italy and ex-Yugoslavia; three collections published of poetry and translations from Italian and Serbian.

Howard, Mavis (*Opening a Window - 1974*) -taught EFL and ESL in Oxford; "in 1974 I was privileged to have in my class some of the wonderful Chilean refugees ... many of whom had been tortured and imprisoned by the Pinochet junta which overthrew the elected government of President Allende."

Ivanova, Teodora (*English & I*) - a pupil at the English Language School, Vidin, Bulgaria.

Jacobson, Jeremy (*The Post-Modern Lecture*) - from Cornwall, currently with the British Council in Bucharest, Romania; he previously worked in Chile; speaks Spanish, Romanian and Cornish.

James, Laurence (*English for Domestic Purposes*) - taught English in Germany and more recently ESL and EAP to many nationalities in UK; now lives in West Wales; has published poetry linked to song in booklets and magazines.

Jiménez Martín, Ana (*A Trip without End*) - a student at the British Institute for Young Learners, Madrid.

Jordan, R.R. (Bob) (*The Idiomatic English Teacher*) - has taught EFL in Finland, Denmark, more recently with the British Council in Nepal and Sierra Leone; lecturer at University of Manchester; published several books in the field of English for Academic Purposes' co-author with Gerry Abbott of *English all over the Place* (forthcoming) which includes a section on well-known writers who were also TEFLers.

Kat Kawel, Georgette (*Lying, In Memory of Tshijik Charnelle, A Smile*) - Congolese student at the University of Westminster, UK: "my inspiration comes from my life experience in the South East of Congo, Lubumbashi".

Kay, John (*Moshav, Students, It Wouldn't Do*) - won first prize in the competition; recently teaching in Saudi-Arabia;

Keith, Rosemary (*Animal Crackers*) - EFL teacher and marriage counselling tutor from Sussex, England' partly Cornish., Scottish, French, Spanish & Basque; her poem "grew out of my teaching experience and counselling observations ... an example of British avoidance of concrete speech, which always confuses foreigners."

Kerr, David (*Other Languages*) - Professor of Theatre, University of Botswana; has published poetry, a novel, stories and books on popular African theatre, media and Dance.

King, Jenny (*Lesson*) - is based in Sheffield.

Kokushkina, Cathy (*Seasons*) - schoolgirl from Sofia, Bulgaria; 9 years old when she wrote the poem after learning English for 5 years; "writing has just been introduced to her, so she cannot have typed this letter but that is all the assistance I have provided"(her mother, E. Tarasheva.).

Lawson, Sarah - originally from Indianapolis, now a long-time Londoner; translates Spanish, French and Dutch; taught at Suzhou University, Jiangsen Province, China, which inspired poems in her collection *Down where the Willow is Washing her Hair.*

Liddy, John (*Language Lesson*) - from Limerick in Ireland; British Council Librarian in Madrid, Spain; his poetry has been published widely in Ireland and Spain; he encouraged a remarkable group of entries to the EFL poetry competition from the British Institute for Young Learners, Madrid.

Luongo Stein, Dona (*"Und So Weiter", In Munich*) - runner-up in the competition; her work widely published in text and multimedia; poems presented with painters, dancers, composer/musicians; two poetry collections published - *Children of the Mafiosi* and *Heavenly Bodies*; she lives in California, USA.

Masopustová, Hana (*The Jail in North Bohemia*) - lives in Ústí nad Labem, Czech Republic.

Mackay, Colin (*The Man with the Umbrella*) - is a poet and novelist living in Edinburgh; *Cold Night Lullaby* (Chapman Publishing, 1998), from which the poem is taken, is based on personal experience as an aid worker during the civil war in Bosnia.

McLaughlin, Jane (*Exile*) - freelance trainer/consultant based in London; when teaching creative writing to native- and non-native speakers, she uses poetry to foster both language development and creativity.

McMahon, Olivia (*English Language Conference in Dublin, Learning a Language, The Visiting Author, As Teacher, as Learner*) - has organised EAP courses at Aberdeen University has taught one-to-one EFL to oil engineers; trained teachers in Sudan, Egypt, Poland, Hungary and Ethiopia; published two EFL textbooks for French speakers.

McNeill, Christine (*Words in his Pocket*) - a widely published poet living in Norfolk.

Michelson, Joan (*Lessons in Humanity [1973-1998]*) - is based in London.

Milošević, Bojana (*I'm Just a Little Girl*) - a student at the English Teaching Centre, Cacak, Yugoslavia; aged 14 when she wrote the poem, sent in by her teacher, Svetlana Lukovic.

Morgan, Edwin (*The First Men on Mercury*) - one of Scotland's most brilliant and versatile poets; in addition to much original poetry, he has also translated poems from various languages.

Mortimore, Roger (*Touch it Again, Sam*) - teaches in Madrid, Spain.

Muñoz Lobo, Miguel Ángel (*About Getting the Exact Word in English*) - a student at the British Institute for Young Learners, Madrid.

Munro, James (*Silent Learner, Helen, You, and Me*) - teaches English in Athens, Greece.

Nicholson, Sarah (*Renewing my Contract*) - is based in London.

Ndlovu, Dumisani Sally (*The Maze*) - lives in Bulawayo, Zimbabwe.

Oxley, Heather (*Poetry Hour*) - teaches and runs creative writing workshops with the British Council in Naples, Italy.

Panowicz, Anna (*Waves and Sand*) - is a young student at International House, Bydgoszcz, Poland; her poem is "a very private poem .. I like to share my passions with others. It might be dangerous, about their reactions. I love to wake up different feelings, different thoughts, in them... lyrics, all about the real emotions, real us. Elements - water, earth. Just like us."

Petit, Susan (*Warra Cheek, The Coffee Bar*) - from County Durham, now living in Rouen, France, where she teaches for the chamber of commerce.

Pikturnienė, Ingrida (*English in Autumn*) - a student with the British Council in Vilnius, Lithuania.

Plavan, Valerian (*Four Seasons*) - lives in Nagano, Japan.

Prentice, N (*Yoshiko*) - teaches EFL part-time at University of Warwick; poems published in various mainstream poetry magazines.

Ramsden, Mike (*Doing "Used to": a Bad Day at the Chalk Face, Evacuation, Invigilating at the Palace, Poetry as a Foreign Language, Practising the Present*) - has taught in various Middle Eastern countries; he is currently based in Muscat Oman.

Rautavuoma, Veera (*Chris*) - is from Jyväskylä, Finland.

Rhyhänen, Merja (*A New World*) - born in Finland, she grew up in Kenya, Liberia and Britain; now works in Finland as a translator; she has "always enjoyed reading and writing enormously ... writing poems and essays was a natural part of school life ... writing still plays a part ... with a full-time job and three kids to raise and a household to run, instead of the earlier desire for lavish forms of expression, I find myself seeking to economise with words without loss in content, bringing my heart ever closer to poetry."

Rossi, Cecilia (*May Poem, Slug*) - is from Buenos Aires, Argentina.

Sandhu, HS (*Stressing the Importance of English*) - teacher of English in India currently studying in Britain; "I adore English poetry, but equally enjoy Urdu and Punjabi poetry, especially "Ghazals" that have no Western equivalent or parallel ... I marvel at my good fortune for having survived this long with a language (English) I am still struggling to learn!"

Schaller, Edigne G (*Le Rose et le Rouge, Learics*) - teaches English and Latin in Olching, Germany; she uses rhymes and limericks with here teaching.

Scrivener, Jim (*Wolves, The Importance of Socks, Proof, "So I'm the Waiter - Order Now"*) - teaches at International House, Budapest, Hungary.

Seatter, Robert (*The Bright Dresses, English Lesson*) - widely published poet and winner of several competitions; taught EFL in Italy and France; worked in ELT publishing and as actor and journalist; now with BBC World Service.

Snuviškienė, Genovaitė (*In a Small English Room*) - teaches English in Vilnius, Lithuania.

Soriano Flórez, Irene (*The White Room*) - a student at the British Institute for Young Learners, Madrid.

Spatoloni, Luciana (*Silent Words*) - teaches English at a high school in Rome; studied flamenco and art; won poetry competitions in Italy and Ireland; recited poems in theatres "accompanying the most flaming ones with flamenco music and dance". "It is easy to learn 'Nice to meet you' and 'What is your name?' But it is difficult to get to the core of the language where the heart beats with emotions and words."

Spiro, Jane (*Englyn and other Words, Time off Summer School, Istanbul*)- one of the competition judges; has taught literature and language for teacher development worldwide, based in Plymouth; prize-winning poet and violinist who has recently completed her first novel.

Swan, Michael (*There are Many Complication, I can Make myself Understood, He Knows Word, Meditation in a Lecture on, For Louis J..., Killed in a Car Crash*) - author of major EFL courses and reference materials; poetry published in magazines and competition anthologies; based in Oxfordshire.

Taher, Su (*Brain Waves*) - lives in Cairo, Egypt.

Tate, Leslie Stuart (*ESOL*) - is based in London.

Treitel, Caroline (*A Lesson in Love*) - is based in London.

Vanderpump, Edward (*Two Loves, The Emperor's Vases, From "The Spoken English of Iraq"*) - taught EFL and ESL in Britain, Germany, Spain, Italy; more recently at Bell School in Norwich; worked in publishing and with computer-assisted language-learning; now a freelance editor and archivist.

Venola, Riitta (*A Special Case, Roofs*) - lives in Pieksämäki, Finland.

Vermes, Vivienne (*The English Lesson*) - writer, actress and broadcaster living in Paris; has published widely - poetry, short stories, non-fiction; winner of Piccadilly Poets Competition, 1997.

Webster, Len (*The Visiting Linguist*) - taught language and literature in Turkey and South-East Asia; lectures in TEFL at City College, Birmingham; author of two published novels and a collection of short-stories.

Widdowson, H.G. (*English Lesson*) - now teaches at Vienna University after a distinguished career in applied linguistics at Edinburgh University and the Institute of Education, London University; has published many influential books and articles on linguistics and language-teaching.

Willock, Susan (*St Mary's Allotments*) - teaches English, History and ESL in East London; worked with Palestinian refugees and in Botswana, where she edited an English magazine and poetry anthology.

INDEX OF TITLES